Prayers OF THE Pious

OMAR SULEIMAN

KUBE
PUBLISHING

In association with

YAQEEN™
INSTITUTE FOR ISLAMIC RESEARCH

Prayers of the Pious

First published in England by
Kube Publishing Ltd
Markfield Conference Centre
Ratby Lane, Markfield
Leicestershire, LE67 9SY
United Kingdom

Tel: +44 (0) 1530 249230
Fax: +44 (0) 1530 249656

Website: www.kubepublishing.com
Email: info@kubepublishing.com

Cataloguing in-Publication Data is available from the British Library.

ISBN 978-1-84774-129-5 *Casebound*
ISBN 978-1-84774-130-1 Ebook

Cover design, illustration and typesetting: Jannah Haque
Printed by: IMAK Ofset, Turkey.

Transliteration Guide

A brief guide to some of the letters and symbols used in the Arabic transliteration in this book.

th	ث	*ḥ*	ح	*dh*	ذ
ṣ	ص	*ḍ*	ض	*ṭ*	ط
ẓ	ظ	ʿ	ع	ʾ	ء

ā	ﺎَ ﮐَ	*ī*	ﻲِ	*ū*	ﻮُ

ﷺ May the peace and blessings of Allah be upon him.

Contents

Introduction

There is a great scholar by the name of Muhammad al-Mukhtar al-Shinqiti *(may Allah be pleased with him)* who once made a very profound comment. He said that people had reached a point in their ignorance of Allah that they don't even call out to Him anymore; they don't know how to have a personal conversation with God. If you think about what a personal *duʿāʾ* looks like, the word in Arabic is *munājāt (intimate conversation)*, Allah *(glorified and exalted is He)* doesn't care if it rhymes, or how it sounds, or even in what language you call out to Him. It doesn't matter, what's important is how sincere it is.

Imam Ahmad *(may Allah be pleased with him)* was once asked, what is the distance between us and the throne of God? A pious prayer from a pure heart, was his reply, that's how we connect to Allah *(glorified and exalted is He)*. When we look at the Prophetic prescriptions of prayers, the best prayers and the best supplications are the ones taught to us by the Qur'an, by the Divine revelation and by the Prophet *(peace be upon him)*, who encouraged the people around him to learn to call upon Allah *(glorified and exalted is He)* in a personal way. If you look at the Companions of the Prophet *(peace be upon him)*, they are essentially a generation of *yaqīn*, of certainty; they are a generation of being connected to Allah *(glorified and exalted is He)* in their own unique ways.

This book, Prayers of the Pious, developed out of a series of lessons that I recorded as part of the Yaqeen Institute during Ramadan in 2018. Each day, I took a prayer from one of our pious predecessors, mostly from the Companions, and taught how to call upon our Creator the same way that they called upon Him. By following this series on a daily basis each month, and by starting to record a personal *du'ā'* journal, writing down your own prayers following the same manner that the pious predecessors used, you can hopefully connect to Allah in the same way they connected to Him. So I hope that you will join me on this journey, and share the Prayers of the Pious and your own prayers with everyone that you know, and please remember to also keep us in your prayers.

Omar Suleiman
March 2019

1

The Best of My Days

اللَّهُمَّ اجْعَلْ خَيْرَ زَمَانِي آخِرَهُ، وَخَيْرَ عَمَلِي خَوَاتِمَهُ،
وَخَيْرَ أَيَّامِي يَوْمَ أَلْقَاكَ

Allāhumma ijʿal khayra zamānī ākhirahu, wa-khayra
ʿamalī khawātimahu, wa-khayra ayyāmī yawma alqāka

O Allah, let the best of my lifetime be its ending,
and my best deed be that which I seal (my life with),
and the best of my days the Day I meet You.

——— ✦ ———

A constantly recurring theme is that the pious predecessors, the Salaf, deliver the most righteous and most beautiful prayers towards the end of their lives. Abū Bakr *(may Allah be pleased with him)* was a man that would give his life for the Prophet *(peace be upon him)*, and he accompanied him in life and in death. He is buried right next to the Prophet *(peace be upon him)*, who mentioned that Abū Bakr would enter into Jannah beside him. You can imagine how much Abū Bakr *(may Allah be pleased with him)* desired to be with the Prophet *(peace be upon him)* after he passed away; how much he looked to the signs of approval and the signs of continuity of what the Prophet *(peace be upon him)* impressed upon him after he departed from this world.

Abū Bakr *(may Allah be pleased with him)* was blessed with an exquisite ending. He was blessed to die on the same day of the week and at the same age that the Prophet *(peace be upon him)* passed away, the age of sixty-three. This was also the same age that ʿUmar and ʿAli *(may Allah be pleased with them)* both died. He took comfort in this knowledge, and he dressed himself as the Prophet *(peace be upon him)* dressed as he was about to pass away. Abū Bakr *(may Allah be pleased with him)* called out with this moving *duʿā*: 'O Allah, let the best of my lifetime be its ending'. What a magnificent life this man had lived but he still said that the best of his life should be its ending. He continued, 'and my best deed be the one that I seal my life with.' Abū Bakr *(may Allah be pleased with him)* had an impressive list of achievements, but his wish was that his best deed be the one that ends his life. And he completed the *duʿāʾ* by saying, 'and let the best of my days be the Day that I meet You,' meaning to meet Allah *(glorified and exalted is He)* on the Day of Judgement.

This is a powerful and alluring *duʿāʾ*. When he passed away, Abū Bakr mentioned the *duʿāʾ* of Prophet Yusuf *(may Allah bless him and grant him peace)*:

تَوَفَّنِي مُسْلِمًا وَأَلْحِقْنِي بِالصَّـٰلِحِينَ.

Let me die a Muslim and be accompanied by the righteous. (Yusuf 12:101)

This is an admirable way for all of us to call upon Allah *(glorified and exalted is He)* because it encompasses the last of our days in terms of time, the last of our deeds to the very specificity of that last deed, and the last of our days, the Day that we meet with Allah *(glorified and exalted is He)*, being the best Day of our life.

Abu Bakr رضي الله عنه
*had an impressive
list of achievements
but his wish was that
his best deed be the
one that ends his life.*

2

His Door Is Always Open

إِلَهِي غَارَتِ النُّجُوْمُ، وَنَامَتِ العُيُوْنُ وَغَلَّقَتِ المُلُوْكُ أَبْوَابَهَا، وَبَابُكَ مَفْتُوْحٌ، وَخَلَا كُلُّ حَبِيْبٍ بِحَبِيْبِهِ، وَهَذَا مَقَامِي بَيْنَ يَدَيْكَ

*Ilāhī ghārati al-nujūmu, wa-nāmati al-ʿuyūnu
wa-ghallaqati al-mulūku abwābahā, wa-bābuka
maftūḥun, wa-khalā kullu ḥabībin bi-ḥabībihī,
wa-hādhā maqāmī bayna yadayka*

*O Allah, the stars have vanished, the eyes
have slept, the kings have locked their doors, and Your
door remains open. Every lover has found privacy with
their beloved, and here I am standing before You.*

This *du'ā'* was narrated by a very special woman, Habibah al-'Adawiyah *(may Allah have mercy on her)*. She is not one of the Companions but one of the following generations, the pious predecessors. It was her custom, as narrated by 'Abdullah al-Makki and others, that towards the middle of the night, when it became very dark and her time of night prayers arrived, she would head up to the rooftop and would call out to Allah with these powerful words. She would continue to pray, and as the night passed and the time for Fajr arrived, she would continue with her *du'ā'* and would end her night with this supplication:

> *O Allah! Here goes the night departing and here comes the day brightening, and how I wish to know, have you accepted this night from me so that I may congratulate myself, or have you rejected it from me so that I may extend myself condolences. By Your might! This is my commitment for as long as you keep me alive. By Your might! Even if you scold me, I will never leave your door, nor will anything but your generosity and your grace be felt in my heart.*

Hafiz Ibn Rajab stated that you spend your days at the doors of the kings, but at night when the King of all the kings calls upon you, you fail to stand for Him and you fail to reach out and respond, even though He calls upon you wanting to provide for you. This *du'a'* combines the conversation that we have with Allah *(glorified and exalted is He)*, with the hope and fear that He has heard our message. Just as our father Ibrahim *(peace be upon him)* and his son called upon Allah *(glorified and exalted is He)* for acceptance after building the Ka'bah, so Habibah al-'Adawiyah *(may Allah have mercy on her)* asks Allah *(glorified and exalted is He)* that if He accepted it she will celebrate, and if He turns it away then she will extend condolences to herself but at the same time keep on trying. Nothing will ever keep her away from His door and nothing will fill her heart except for His grace and love.

When we call upon Allah *(glorified and exalted is He)* with a very personal *du'a'*, we may say: very well then, we have made our *du'a'* and now we're waiting for some kind of miracle to happen. So we can either become complacent after we have had an amazing conversation with our Lord, or become discouraged and start to move away because something happens the next day that we feel was a sign that our *du'a'*, our supplication, wasn't accepted. We will never know for certain whether our *du'a'* was accepted in this world or not, and the power and the beauty of Habibah al-'Adawiyah's *du'a'* is that all she wanted as the night passed was another opportunity to be at the door of her Lord and she would never give up.

May Allah *(glorified and exalted is He)* never turn us away from His door and may Allah allow us to always be among those that call upon him, and may we knock at that door until we are finally greeted by Him in the Hereafter and welcomed by Him into His gardens. *Āmīn.*

3

A Covenant with Allah

اللَّهُمَّ فَاطِرَ السَّمَاوَاتِ والأَرْضِ، عَالِمَ الغَيْبِ وَالشَّهَادَةِ، إِنِّي أَعْهَدُ إِلَيْكَ في هَذِهِ الحَيَاةِ الدُّنْيَا: إِنَّكَ إِنْ تَكِلْني إِلَى نَفْسِي تُقَرِّبُني مِنْ الشَّرِّ، وَتُبَاعِدُني مِنْ الخَيْرِ، وإِنِّي إِنْ أَثِقُ إِلَّا بِرَحْمَتِكَ فَاجْعَلْهُ لي عِنْدَكَ عَهْدَاً تُؤَدِّهِ إِلَيَّ يَوْمَ القِيَامَةِ، إِنَّكَ لَا تُخْلِفُ المِيْعَادَ

Allāhumma fātira al-samāwāti wal-arḍi, ‘ālima al-ghaybi wal-shahādati, innī a‘hadu ilayka fī hādhihi al-ḥayāti al-dunya: innaka in takilnī ilā nafsī tuqarribunī mina al-sharri, wa-tubā‘idunī mina al-khayri, wa-innī in athiku illā biraḥmatika faj‘alhu lī ‘indaka ‘ahdan tu’addihī ilayya yawma al-qiyāmati, innaka lā-tukhlifu al-mī‘ād

O Allah, Originator of the heavens and earth, Knower of the seen and unseen, I testify in this worldly life of mine that if You leave me to myself, by that You are bringing me closer to harm and distancing me from good. I have no confidence except in Your mercy, so let that be a covenant that You deliver to me on the Day of Judgment—for You never break Your promises.

———— ✦ ————

This *duʿāʾ* is about the covenant that we make with Allah *(glorified and exalted is He)*. Few of the supplications are covenants that you actually make with Allah, and obviously when you make a covenant with Allah—when you take an oath upon Allah—it increases the severity and sometimes the sincerity of that supplication.

It is narrated by Aswad ibn Yazid that ʿAbdullah ibn Masʿūd *(may Allah be pleased with him)* recited the verse

لَا يَمْلِكُونَ الشَّفَاعَةَ إِلَّا مَنِ اتَّخَذَ عِندَ الرَّحْمَٰنِ عَهْدًا

No one will have the power to intercede [with Allah], except for him who has taken a covenant with the All-Beneficent, (Maryam 19:87)

and when he said that, ʿAbdullah ibn Masʿūd said that on the Day of Judgement Allah will say: 'Whoever has a covenant with Me, then let him stand.' The students of 'Abdullah ibn Mas'ūd *(may Allah be pleased with him)* asked him to teach them what to do with that, what to say about that. This is a situation where you actually have a *Sahabi (a Companion)* like Ibn Mas'ūd teaching his students what to say. So this particular *du'ā'* has many blessings in that sense.

One of the questions about the Qur'an is how do you interact with those verses? The Prophet *(peace be upon him)* said of 'Abdullah ibn Mas'ūd, 'whoever wants to hear the Qur'an fresh, as if it was just recited, then let him listen to the qira'at of 'Abdullah ibn Mas'ūd'. And this is how he interacts with this particular verse and this idea of taking a covenant with Allah *(glorified and exalted is He)*. One of the things that we learn about Allah *(glorified and exalted is He)* is that He is too shy to turn away the hands of His sincere servants. So when you call upon Allah and you say, 'O Allah! You never break your promises. You promised us mercy, so please show us mercy; You promised that if we do this, You will do that.' It's a very beautiful and powerful way to engage your *Rabb*, to engage your Lord, to engage your Sustainer. A Lord that loves to forgive, a Lord that loves to pardon, a Lord that loves to show mercy.

May Allah *(glorified and exalted is He)* deliver us on the Day of Judgement, as He promised us that if we believe in Him and we turn to Him and obey Him to the best of our ability that He will deliver us with His mercy. May Allah *(glorified and exalted is He)* deliver us with His mercy and allow us to enter into the Gardens of felicity.

4

The Enormity of My Sins
— VS —
His Mercy

يَا رَبِّ إِنَّ ذُنُوْبِي عَظِيْمَةٌ، وَإِنَّ قَلِيْلَ عَفْوِكَ أَعْظَمُ مِنْهَا، اللَّهُمَّ فَامْحُ بِقَلِيْلِ عَفْوِكَ عَظِيْمَ ذُنُوْبِي

Ya rabbi inna dhunūbī ʿaẓimatun, wa-inna qalīla ʿafwika aʿẓamu minhā, allāhumma famḥu bi-qalīli ʿafwika ʿaẓīma dhunūbī

My Lord, my sins are enormous, but a little
of Your forgiveness is greater than all of them.
O Allah, so erase with a little of Your forgiveness
the enormity of my sins.

In an era where the hero is not always a hero and the villain is not always a villain, the subject of this *du'ā'*, unlike many other figures in this series, is an incredibly complex character. His name is 'Abd al-Malik ibn Marwan *(may Allah be pleased with him)* and he was the fifth Umayyad caliph, who accomplished many great things in Islamic history. But he was not perfect, and often when you're looking at these complex characters, you don't want to completely deny their achievements but at the same time you cannot close your eyes to their flaws. He was self-aware of his flaws and he recognized the complexity of the situation. He made this *du'ā'*, this supplication, at the end of his life, and al-Asma'i *(may Allah be pleased with him)* actually said that he envied Ibn Marwan to be able to make that supplication at the end of his life for the beauty of the words that he makes.

The *du'ā'* is really interesting because there is no boasting on 'Abd al-Malik ibn Marwan's part. It is an acknowledgement of vulnerability, of weakness; this is laying it bare, as you should do with *du'ā'*. You should be very personal and very emotional with Allah *(glorified and exalted is He)* and acknowledge your flaws and vulnerabilities. If you look at all of the supplications of the Prophet *(peace be upon him)*, particularly in the context of istighfar and seeking forgiveness, there is always acknowledgement.

As they say in istighfar, 'I admit Your blessings upon me and I admit my sins'. Here, 'Abd al-Malik ibn Marwan is acknowledging a very important point in the *du'ā'* that you will not enter Jannah because of your good deeds, or because of the greatness of your good deeds or the lack of your sins. You will enter Jannah on the basis of your efforts and qualifying for the mercy of Allah *(glorified and exalted is He)*, and we are all in need of the mercy of Allah.

If you think about this life, the Prophet *(peace be upon him)* says that of the one hundred parts of Allah's mercy, all of them have been reserved for the Hereafter except for one. So all the mercy and compassion that you see in this world, all that comes out of that one part of Allah's mercy and the rest of it all is reserved for the Hereafter. Imagine what type of a Lord you have, how Merciful, *al-Rahmān (the Most Beneficent), al-Rahīm (the Most Compassionate)* He actually is. If you can acknowledge this, and we should be hopeful at the end of our lives, but hope should not excuse us or cause us to run away from our obligations and responsibilities. It should be acknowledged that it was never about 'me' in the first place, O Allah, it is about Your mercy, and we should recognize and acknowledge that a little bit of His mercy is enough to handle the entirety of our sins.

May Allah *(glorified and exalted is He)* forgive us for our sins, the big ones and the small ones, the public ones and the private ones, the ones we recognize and the ones we fail to recognize. *Āmīn.*

❧ 5 ❧

The Hand
That Kills Me

اللَّهُمَّ ارْزُقْنِي شَهَادَةً فِي سَبِيلِكَ وَاجْعَلْ مَوْتِي فِي بَلَدِ رَسُوْلِكَ صَلَّى اللهُ عَلَيْهِ وَسَلَّمَ. اللَّهُمَّ لَا تَجْعَلْ قَتْلِي عَلَى يَدِ عَبْدٍ سَجَدَ لَكَ سَجْدَةً يُحَاجُّنِي بِهَا يَوْمَ القِيَامَةِ.

Allāhumma urzuqnī shahādatan fī sabīlika waj'al mawtī fī balādi rasūlika ṣalla Allahu 'alayhi wa-sallam. Allahuma lā-taj'al qatlī 'alā yadi 'abdin sajada laka sajdatan yuḥājjunī bihā yawma al-qiyāmah

O Allah, I ask You, to be accepted as a martyr in the city of your Prophet (peace and blessings of Allah be upon him). O Allah, do not let my killing be at the hand of someone who ever prostrated to You, lest he use that against me on the Day of Judgement.

In the first *du'ā'* we discussed the death of Abū Bakr *(may Allah be pleased with him)* and how he longed for the last of his deeds and the last of his days to be the best, and the best moment to be when he meets Allah *(glorified and exalted is He)*. Now, consider the situation of 'Umar *(may Allah be pleased with him)*; imagine knowing that you are going to be killed and that your ending is going to be murder. 'Umar would know this is the case because the Prophet *(peace be upon him)* was with him and Abū Bakr and 'Uthman *(may Allah be pleased with them)* on Mount Uhud and it shook. The Prophet *(peace be upon him)* said, 'Be firm O Uhud! You have upon you a Prophet (himself), a *ṣiddīq* (Abū Bakr) and two martyrs (meaning 'Umar and 'Uthman)'. So 'Umar *(may Allah be pleased with him)* was well aware that he will be martyred, but that wasn't enough for him. He knew that he was guaranteed Jannah because the Prophet *(peace be upon him)* mentioned 'Umar on numerous occasions as being one who is guaranteed Paradise. He feared hypocrisy, because he would actually ask Hudhayfah *(may Allah be pleased with him)* for the names of hypocrites to know if he was on the list that the Prophet *(peace be upon him)* gave to him, and yet he still made so many *du'ā*'s about the moment that he would be killed, who would kill him, where he would be killed and how he would be killed.

His daughter asked him how he could die a martyr in Madinah, to which he replied that if Allah wanted it to happen, it would happen.

There is a famous *du'ā'* where 'Umar says: 'O Allah! I ask you to be accepted as a martyr in your path, and let that martyrdom take place in the city of your Prophet'. For 'Umar to think that he could be killed in Madinah is unusual, because the Prophet *(peace be upon him)* was obviously settled in Madinah and the Muslims were based in Madinah. So the idea of him being killed in the city of the Prophet *(peace be upon him)* by a Muslim was very unlikely. Indeed, when he used to make that *du'ā'*, his daughter asked him how he could die a martyr in Madinah, to which he replied that if Allah wanted it to happen, it would happen. That this man, who one day went out to kill the Prophet *(peace be upon him)* and became Muslim, would be killed in the city of the Prophet *(peace be upon him)* and be buried next to him, shows that you never know the ending of a person.

'Umar *(may Allah be pleased with him)* also made this *du'ā'*, 'O Allah, do not let my killing be at the hand of someone who ever prostrated to You, lest he uses that against me on the Day of Judgement'. 'Umar *(may Allah be pleased with him)* did not want to be killed by a believer or anyone who had the semblance of righteousness. He didn't want to be killed by someone shouting *Allāhu akbar* or *lā ilāha illa Allāh*. In fact, when 'Umar was stabbed, he was leading the prayer in the Mosque of the Prophet *(peace be upon him)*, and the first question he asked was whether the person who stabbed him was a Muslim. When he learned that the killer was not a Muslim, he said *Alhamdulillah* that his ending didn't come at the hands of a believer.

It's telling that 'Umar *(may Allah be pleased with him)* was so detached from this world and so attached to the gardens of Jannah that he had already included all of this in his supplication. He asked Allah *(glorified and exalted is He)* that he should die in the city of the Prophet *(peace be upon him)*, and the Prophet said whoever is sincere and asking for *shahādah (martyrdom)* could die a martyr even in their bed. So if a person sincerely asks for *shahādah* in his supplication, they will achieve martyrdom whatever the case and circumstance of their death might be. 'Umar *(may Allah be pleased with him)* also asked for *shahādah* in the Prophet's city, and the Prophet *(peace be upon him)* had said, 'whoever amongst you *(the Muslims)* can die in Madinah, let him do so'; meaning that spending as much time in Madinah longing for death there was possible because the Prophet *(peace be upon him)* said he would intercede for the one who has died in Madinah. Finally, in his care and love for this Ummah and his fear of having a believer contest him on the Day of Judgment, he asks Allah *(glorified and exalted is He)* that the person that kills him not be a believer, and Allah granted him all of those unlikely circumstances. He is buried right next to Abū Bakr *(may Allah be pleased with him)* and the Prophet *(peace be upon him)*, so do not underestimate the power of Allah *(glorified and exalted is He)*, as nothing is impossible for the Most Merciful.

6

The Highest Companionship

اللَّهُمَّ إِنِّي أَسْأَلُكَ إِيمَانًا لَا يَرْتَدُّ ، وَنِعِيْمًا لَا يَنْفَدُ، وَمُرَافَقَةَ نَبِيِّكَ مُحَمَّدٍ صَلَّى اللهُ عَلَيْهِ وَسَلَّمَ فِي أَعْلَى جَنَّةِ الْخُلْدِ

Allāhumma innī as'aluka īmānan lā-yartaddu, wa-na'īman lā-yanfadu, wa-murāfaqata nabiyyika Muhammadan ṣalla Allahu 'alayhi wa-sallama fī a'lā jannati al-khuldi

O Allah, I ask You for faith that does not unravel, and delight that never depletes, and the companionship of Your Prophet Muhammad (peace and blessings of Allah be upon him) in the highest eternal garden.

Often, you come across a narration where the Prophet *(peace be upon him)* is walking past someone, or someone's house, or he may see someone in the *masjid* and overhear a supplication, and he actually approves of that supplication or expresses awe. Imagine the scene, therefore, where the Prophet *(peace be upon him)* is walking the streets of Madinah one night with Abū Bakr and ʿUmar *(may Allah be pleased with them)* and through the mosque of the Prophet *(peace be upon him)* and they come across ʿAbdullah ibn Masʿūd *(may Allah be pleased with him)* standing, immersed in his prayers and calling upon Allah *(glorified and exalted is He)* with the most beautiful of recitation. Of course, the recitation of ʿAbdullah ibn Masʿūd was so beloved by the Prophet *(peace be upon him)* that he would ask ʿAbdullah to recite the Qurʾan for him.

These three great men are walking through Madinah and come across this man calling upon Allah *(glorified and exalted is He)*, crying and immersed in his recitation, and then he starts to make his *duʿā'*, his supplication. As he is doing so, the Prophet *(peace be upon him)* stops and listens to the words of his supplication. Then he says, 'Go ahead and ask and you will be given, ask and you will be given'. Abū Bakr and ʿUmar wished that they could have that blessing at that moment. Can you imagine a believer asking from Allah in his *du'ā'* and the Prophet *(peace be upon him)* saying: 'ask and you will be given, ask and you will be given.' 'Abdullah ibn Mas'ūd *(may Allah be pleased with him)* makes his *du'ā'* and at the end of the supplication the Prophet *(peace be upon him)* says, *'Āmīn'*. It doesn't get better than that, and that his *du'ā'* was so precious to 'Abdullah ibn Mas'ūd *(may Allah be pleased with him)*, he said, 'By Allah, I have never prayed a single prayer, not an obligatory prayer nor voluntary prayer except at the end of my salah', it encompasses everything.

Consider the words of the *du'ā'*, 'faith that does not unravel', because nothing should be more beloved to you in this world than your faith, and 'delight that never depletes'. When you ask Allah for Jannah, what do you look for more than anything else? As the Prophet *(peace be upon him)* said, don't just ask for Paradise, ask for the highest level. So 'Abdullah asked Allah *(glorified and exalted is He)* for the companionship of His Prophet Muhammad *(peace be upon him)* in the highest eternal garden. 'Abdullah didn't just want to be in Jannah, or even to be in the highest level of Jannah, but he wanted the companionship of His Prophet *(peace be upon him)*. This was the most precious request of the Companions of the Prophet *(peace be upon him)*, beyond every other request. When the Prophet *(peace be upon him)* asked them what they wanted, all they ever wanted was his companionship in the highest level of Paradise.

May we also ask Allah *(glorified and exalted is He)* for faith that does not unravel, for the delight that never depletes, and for the companionship of the Prophet *(peace be upon him)* in the highest eternal garden of Jannah. *Āmīn.*

7

O Allah, You Know That I Love You

اللَّهُمَّ إِنِّي أَعُوذُ بِكَ مِنْ صَبَاحِ النَّارِ وَمِنْ مَسَائِهَا،
وَلَمَّا نَزَلَ بِهِ المَوْتُ قَالَ: هَذِهِ آخِرُ سَاعَةٍ مِنْ الدُّنْيَا،
اللَّهُمَّ إِنَّكَ تَعْلَمُ أَنِّي أُحِبُّكَ فَبَارِكْ لِي فِي لِقَائِكَ

*Allāhumma innī aʿūdhu bika min ṣabāḥi al-nāri
wa-min masāʾihā, wa-lammā nazala bihī al-mawtu
qāla: hādhihī ākhiru sāʿatin mina al-dunyā, allāhumma
innaka taʿlamu annī uḥibbuka fa-bārik lī fī liqāʾika*

**O Allah, I seek shelter with You from the
mornings and evenings in the Hellfire.
O Allah, this is my last hour in this world. You know
that I certainly love You, so bless my meeting with You.**

When you look at the Companions of the Prophet *(peace be upon him)*, you find a man by the name of Hudhayfah ibn al-Yaman *(may Allah be pleased with him)*, the secret keeper of the Prophet *(peace be upon him)*. He was the one with whom the Prophet *(peace be upon him)* entrusted the name of the hypocrites *(munafiqun)*. Hudhayfah said that people used to ask the Prophet *(peace be upon him)* about the good things, like Jannah, and hopeful things, 'but I used to ask him about evil and evil consequences so that I could avoid those things'.

Hudhayfah used to make this *du'ā' (supplication)*: 'O Allah, I seek shelter with You from the mornings and evenings in the Hellfire', meaning that he did not want to touch the Hellfire in any way whatsoever. He was afraid of punishment and he didn't want to encounter it in any way. When Hudhayfah was about to die, he made this supplication, and one gets goosebumps just thinking about it. He said: 'Oh, Allah. This is my last hour in this world. O Allah, You know that I certainly love You, so bless my meeting with You.'

How much love do you have to have for Allah *(glorified and exalted is He)*, and confidence in that love, as you're departing from this world, that you can say, 'You know how much I love You'. This is a test for all of us, and Imam Ahmad *(may Allah be pleased with him)* said that if you want to know your position before Allah, then look at His position with you. If you want to know how much God loves you then look at how much you love Him. For Hudhayfah to have that confidence, that connection with Allah, he is not just saying that he loves Him but that He knows how much he loves Him, is a very powerful testament to the type of relationship that he had with Allah *(glorified and exalted is He)*. Of course, in our situation the Prophet *(peace be upon him)* told us to say, 'O Allah! I ask You for Your love, and for the love of those who love You and for the love of every action that would bring us closer to Your love.'

So asking Allah *(glorified and exalted is He)* for His love, asking Allah to love us, asking Allah for the love of those that are beloved to Him, asking Allah for the love of those that love Him, and asking Allah for the love of every action that brings us nearer to His love, all of this encompasses us at the end of the day because hope and fear are only the wings, but the love of Allah *(glorified and exalted is He)* is the body and the crux of the matter.

May Allah *(glorified and exalted is He)* allow us to die with certainty that we love Him and we're beloved by

Him, and may Allah make our reunion with Him on the Day of Judgement be a reunion of those that love one another. May Allah *(glorified and exalted is He)* allow us to be gathered together in His love on the Day of Judgement. *Āmīn*.

8

The Precious Prayer of a Mother

اللَّهُمَّ ارْحَمْ طُولَ ذَلِكَ القِيامِ في اللَّيْلِ الطَّويلِ،
وَذَلِكَ النَّحِيْبِ وَالظَّمَأَ في هَوَاجِرِ المَدِيْنَةِ وَمَكَّةَ،
وَبِرَّهُ بِأَبِيْهِ وَبِي. اللَّهُمَّ قَدْ سَلَّمْتُهُ لِأَمْرِكَ فِيْهِ،
وَرَضِيْتُ بِمَا قَضَيْتَ فَأَثِبْنِي في عَبْدِ اللهِ
ثَوَابَ الصَّابِرِيْنَ الشَّاكِرِيْنَ

Allāhumma irḥam ṭūla dhālika al-qiyāmi fī al-layli
al-ṭawīli, wa-dhālika al-naḥībi wal-ẓama'a fī hawājiri
al-madīnati wa-makkah, wa-birrahu bi-abīhi wa-bī.
Allāhumma qad sallamtuhu li-amrika fīh, wa-raḍaytu
bimā qaḍayta fa-athibnī fī ʿabdi Allāhi thawāba
al-ṣābirīn al-shākirīn

O Allah, have mercy on his lengthy standing during the longest nights, and that whimpering, and his thirst during the hot summer days of Makkah and Madinah (all of those days that he starved, all of those days that he suffered, all of those days that he was abandoned and all of those days that he stood up, calling upon You during the longest night), and reward his kindness to his father and to me. O Allah, I have surrendered him to whatever You decree on him, and I have made myself content with whatever You have decided for him. So grant me the reward of the patient and the thankful.

---- ✦ ----

One of the most touching and heartbreaking stories in the *Sīrah* of the Prophet *(peace be upon him)* or his Companions is the story of ʿAbdullah ibn Zubayr *(may Allah be pleased with him)*, the first child to be born in Madinah, who the Muslims carried and chanted *Allāhu akbar,* as he was in the hands of Abū Bakr as-Ṣiddīq *(may Allah be pleased with him)* and the Prophet Muhammad *(peace be upon him)*, to dispel any idea that there was a curse surrounding the women of Madinah and their ability to give birth. He was born in resistance, his birth was resistance, and he died in resistance after his tragic assassination and crucifixion. As ʿAbdullah ibn ʿUmar mentioned, 'I was there on that day when they carried him on the streets of Madinah chanting *Allāhu akbar* as he was born, and I was there on the day that they crucified him, and these ugly people that used the name of Allah were also chanting *Allāhu akbar*, just like those beautiful people who carried him as a child in the streets of Madinah and chanted *Allāhu akbar* as he was given life'.

The people that murdered him chanted *Allāhu akbar* and took joy in his assassination; a very meaningful and powerful moment for us to reflect upon and appreciate the fact that 'Abdullah ibn Zubayr was a person who stood against all the odds. He resisted the oppression of the Caliph, he resisted the oppression from other people, that were saying *lā ilāha illa Allāh Muhammadur-Rasūllullāh (there is no God except Allah and Muhammad is His Prophet)* and now he is standing before his mother, Asma' bint Abū Bakr *(may Allah be pleased with her)*, who was almost a 100 years old at that time. Asma' was one of the first Muslims to deliver food to the Prophet *(peace be upon him)* and kept news of the Prophet and Abū Bakr *(may Allah be pleased with him)* during the migration. She served Islam throughout her life, this woman who was beaten by Abū Jahl because of her service, and now her son is seeking advice from her on how to deal with suppression and she is comforting him and preparing him for that moment where he will

She not only mentioned her son's sacrifices and his service, but she also asked *Allah* for the reward of her own sacrifice and service.

be crucified and killed right next to the house of Allah (*glorified and exalted is He*).

So, she makes this *du'ā'* for him, and there is no greater *du'ā'* than that of a mother and no more powerful a *du'ā'* than that of a person who is under oppression. There are so many themes that we can take from this *du'ā'*, the *du'ā'* of the oppressed, the *du'ā'* of the mother, the love and admiration that this mother had for her own child and what she saw in his standing and whimpering and crying out to Allah (*glorified and exalted is He*); how he struggled his entire life and lived the life of resistance. She not only mentions his sacrifices and his service, but she also asks Allah for the reward of her sacrifice and her service. Perhaps the most important lesson we can take from this is that Asma' was privy to the fact that the death of her son would ultimately lead to her own death as well, as she was living at that point through her son.

When 'Abdullah ibn Zubayr (*may Allah be pleased with him*) was crucified, he was left crucified next to the Ka'bah, and she would come out, this 100-year-old woman, and cry at his body and ask: 'Isn't it time for this noble warrior to come down. Isn't it time for this body, this man to be honoured?' She pleaded until eventually his body was taken down, and she died only a few days later. May Allah *(glorified and exalted is He)* be pleased with her and allow us to meet this beautiful woman, this powerful mother, who is a symbol of resistance, a symbol of righteousness in all circumstances, on the Day of Judgement.

May Allah *(glorified and exalted is He)* be pleased with her son and be pleased with her family and May Allah allow us to face our oppressors with the greatest courage and great sincerity and be families that are thankful and patient even in the most difficult days. *Āmīn.*

❧ 9 ❧

The Greed of the Soul

اللَّهُمَّ قِنِي شُحَّ نَفْسِي

Allāhumma qinī shuḥḥa nafsī

O Allah, protect me from the greed of my soul!

---------- ✦ ----------

Sometimes, when you look at the fears of the prophets and of the Companions and the righteous, you see that they feared things that don't make sense to us. They were good at many things and they were so distant from the evil traits that they feared that we cannot understand why they feared these things, be they physical or emotional. For example, Ibrahim *(may Allah be pleased with him)* is called *al-Ṣiddīq (the truthful one)* but he feared dishonesty; Maryam *(may Allah be pleased with her)* is the most modest and the greatest and purest of all women, but she still feared immodesty, perhaps more than anything else. This speaks of the high standards of these people and the standards that they set for themselves.

Perhaps the richest Companion that you could think of is ʿAbd al-Rahman ibn ʿAwf *(may Allah be pleased with him)*. He was known for his utmost generosity and would bring caravans to Madinah that were so great that the people of Madinah would think that the city was under occupation or that an army was attacking. He constantly gave and gave so that he could make a case to Allah *(glorified and exalted is He)* to not only provide in this world but by his generosity would also to allow him to enter into Paradise. He was observed making this one supplication during tawaf, over and over again, and he would not do anything else. Imagine this generous man walking around the Kaʿbah seven times and the only *duʿāʾ* he makes is: 'O Allah, protect me from the greed of my soul!'

When he was asked why he would make only that *duʿāʾ*, he replied, 'if I'm protected from the greed of my soul then I would not steal, I would not commit adultery, and I would not do anything evil'. First and foremost, there is greed in the obvious sense: that a person becomes greedy with his money so they start to cheat and take advantage of people, and exploit other people even when there is no need. As the Prophet *(peace be upon him)* said, if the son of Adam is given a valley of gold, he will want another valley of gold, and if he is given two valleys of gold then he will want to have three valleys of gold. He will never be satisfied until he has dirt in his mouth, meaning that he would continue to want more and more until there was nothing left.

So that's one form of greed, but ʿAbd al-Rahman ibn ʿAwf is also talking about a person with spiritual poverty, who is just like one with financial poverty and starts to exploit people. Of course, we are not talking about the genuinely poor, but those people who have plenty but who always feel as if they are in poverty when they are not, hence they want more and start doing things that are unethical and wrong. This is what ʿAbd al-Rahman ibn ʿAwf *(may Allah be pleased with him)* is talking about, we sin out of a feeling of emptiness and we sin when there is a void that's not properly being filled. Often, the same emotion that triggers exploitation in the financial sense allows a person to do things that are well beyond the bounds of decency, for themselves and their souls.

So this is a *du'ā'* that we should learn and say, whether that greed is financial or emotional. We should seek protection from anything that would cause us to transgress and to desire or to try to attain more than what Allah *(glorified and exalted is He)* has written for us in a way that is not pleasing to Him.

❧ 10 ❧

A Prayer More Powerful than the Wind

أَرَيْتَنَا قُدْرَتَكَ فَأَرِنَا عَفْوَكَ

Araytanā qudrataka fa-arinā ʿafwaka

**You have shown us Your power,
so show us Your forgiveness.**

———— ✦ ————

Some of us may have actually been in this scenario, and you can probably relate to the story of Yunus *(peace be upon him)*, but imagine being on a boat or a ship and the waves start to crash and the wind starts to blow hard and you think you are about to fall off the ship and drown. The ocean is a terrifying place and it's a very difficult situation to be in, and it's such a powerful analogy to the story of Yunus *(peace be upon him)* that you know what it feels like to be in those moments.

Imam al-Dhahabi *(may Allah be pleased with him)* narrates a story from the life of the great scholar Ibrahim ibn Adham *(may Allah be pleased with him)*. He was a sage, a scholar and an incredible human being whose righteousness was recognized by everyone around him. One time Ibrahim ibn Adham was on a ship, sleeping, and the winds became enraged, the waves started to crash against the ship and everybody on board was certain that they were going to die. As the storm grew severe and ship started to rock left and right, Ibrahim ibn Adham rose from his sleep and went on deck. The people around him thought they were all going to die, and they asked, 'O father of Ishāq *(his eldest son's name)* what can you call upon Allah with now to save us from this situation!' He rose and raised his hands to the sky and said: 'O You Ever-living One! O Ever Sustaining One! You have shown us Your power, so show us Your pardon *(your forgiveness)*.'

As soon as he made that *du'ā'*, everything calmed down; the wind calmed and the waves settled and the ship sailed on smoothly. In fact, Ibrahim ibn Adham lay down and went back to sleep, and that's the

Remember a time when you really witnessed the power of Allah and you could see how completely and utterly dependent we are on Him.

connection that the man had with Allah (*glorified and exalted is He*). Now, focus on the main theme of this *du'ā'*, instead of just thinking how amazing was Ibrahim bin Adham, and remember a time when you really witnessed the power of Allah (*glorified and exalted is He*), and you can see how completely and utterly dependent we are on Him. Ibrahim ibn Adham didn't say 'You've shown us your punishment', he said, 'You've shown us Your power,' and this was a manifestation of His power, and then he said, 'now show us Your pardon'. Pardon is beyond mercy and forgiveness, it's when we're left alone and safe.

The next time you find yourself in a desperate situation, and you may be in such a situation right now, when you find yourself completely dependent on Allah (*glorified and exalted is He*) call upon Him and say, 'O Allah! I am a witness to Your power, now I want You to show me Your mercy and Your pardon, and to show us Your safety'.

May Allah (*glorified and exalted is He*) always grant us His pardon and safety, just as He always shows us that power and allows us to witness that power and mercy in this world and in the Hereafter. *Āmīn.*

11

Don't Punish a Tongue of Praise

إِلَهِي لَا تُعَذِّبْ لِسَاناً يُخْبِرُ عَنْكَ، وَلَا عَيْناً تَنْظُرُ إِلَى عُلُومٍ تَدُلُّ عَلَيْكَ، وَلَا يَداً تَكْتُبُ حَدِيثَ رَسُولِكَ؛ فَبِعِزَّتِكَ لَا تُدْخِلَنِي النَّارَ

Ilāhī lā-tuʿadhib lisānan yukhbiru ʿanka, wa-lā ʿaynan tanzuru ilā ʿulūmin tadullu ʿalayka, wa-lā yadan taktubu ḥadītha rasūlika; fabiʿizzatika lā-tudkhilanī al-nār

My God, do not punish a tongue that informs about You, nor an eye that looks upon (Islamic) sciences which point to You, nor a hand that writes the Traditions of Your Messenger. So by Your honour, do not admit me into the Fire.

Imam Ibn al-Jawzi *(may Allah be pleased with him)* was a great teacher and scholar who lived centuries after the Prophet *(peace be upon him)*. He would tell his students, if you make it to Jannah and you don't find me then ask about me, and ask Allah *(glorified and exalted is He)* to enter me into Jannah as well. Imam Ibn al-Jawzi had sessions with thousands of people at a time, and he would cry out to Allah *(glorified and exalted is He)* and say, 'O Allah! Do not punish me, because if you punish me people will say that Allah punished the one that used to teach us about him'.

His argument in his *du'ā*'s and pleas to Allah *(glorified and exalted is He)*, like this one, were born out of a fear of hypocrisy: I'm teaching people about You, so don't humiliate me because then they will say that Allah humiliated the one who taught them about Him. I'm guiding people to Jannah, I'm acting as an ultimate instrument of guidance, but if I do things or say things that are not pleasing to You that might cause me to be punished, don't let it be that people show up in Jannah and they don't find the one who taught them about You. This is one of the things we learn from the Prophet *(peace be upon him)*, to invoke Allah *(glorified and exalted is He)* with our good deeds; not out of arrogance but out of humility.

When you are invoking Allah *(glorified and exalted is He)* recognize your shortcomings, or realize that you might not be the best of people and you need to rectify those flaws that you need to overcome. Become an instrument of guidance to His gardens, and out of His generosity and benevolence and honour, Allah will not enter you into the Fire.

May Allah *(glorified and exalted is He)* allow all of us to be beneficial to others without losing ourselves, and may He guide us and guide through us, and rectify our hearts and rectify other people's hearts and through us help to rectify others. May Allah *(glorified and exalted is He)* allow us to enter His Paradise by His mercy and accept our good deeds and forgive our sins. *Āmīn.*

We learn from the Prophet ﷺ to invoke Allah with our good deeds; not out of arrogance but out of humility.

12

Don't Make an Example Out of Me

اللَّهُمَّ لَا تَجْعَلْني عِبْرَةً لِغَيْرِي، وَلَا تَجْعَلْ أَحَداً أَسْعَدَ بِمَا عَلَّمْتَني مِنِّي

Allāhumma lā-tajʿalnī ʿibratan li-ghayrī, wa-lā tajʿal aḥadan asʿada bimā ʿallamtanī minnī

O Allah, do not make a lesson out of me for others, and do not let there be anyone who benefits more than me from what You have taught me.

In the previous *du'ā'* we learned about Imam Ibn al-Jawzi *(may Allah be pleased with him)* and his fear that even though he was a source of guidance to his students that Allah *(glorified and exalted is He)* would still punish him for his flaws and the teacher would not be present in Paradise. There is another *du'ā'* by another great man, al-Mutarrif ibn 'Abdullah *(may Allah be pleased with him)*, that speaks of this fear from another angle. In his *du'ā'*, al-Mutarrif ibn 'Abdullah addresses his shortcomings and asks that Allah *(glorified and exalted is He)* does not punish him and make an example out of him for others, obviously speaking in regards to sin. And then he asks that whatever he has taught others, he can practically benefit more from that knowledge than anyone else.

This is a powerful way of expressing similar sentiments as Ibn al-Jawzi *(may Allah be pleased with him)*. The Prophet *(peace be upon him)* mentioned that some lands absorb the revelations like water on fertile soil, where water is taken up and produces that which is beneficial, and the people benefit. Sometimes the revelations hit a hard surface, and neither the surface nor the people around benefit. And sometimes it's like a bowl, or land that is shaped in a certain way, and even though that land does not absorb the revelation, the water remains in place and still provides benefit to others. However, we don't want to be just vessels for others, we want to be like the fertile soil that is able to absorb the knowledge and teach others.

These men and women were very aware of this idea of not being made an example of hypocrisy, shortcoming and being a sinner for others to see. But at the same time, they did not want others to benefit more from their knowledge than themselves: Let me benefit the most from the knowledge that I'm imparting to others, because you don't want to be seen as someone who completely forgoes the practice of what he preaches. This is what Allah means in the Qur'an when He says,

> 'You who believe, why do you say things and then do not do them? It is most hateful to God that you say things and then do not do them'. (al-Saff 61: 2–3)

Hence one should be attempting more than anyone else in what one teaches and practice more of it than others are privy to, and not simply preach for the sake of it. Always ask Allah *(glorified and exalted is He)* to give you beneficial knowledge and just as you are a source of guidance for others that you yourself do not go astray.

May Allah *(glorified and exalted is He)* make us among those who learn and benefit from what is correct, teach others that which is correct and that we will enter Jannah with those who are righteous, not just as people of knowledge but as worshippers and people who acted upon that knowledge as well. *Āmīn*.

❧ 13 ❧

A Station
of Patience
Without Trial

اللَّهُمَّ إِنْ كُنْتَ بَلَغْتَ أَحَداً مِنْ عِبَادِكَ الصَّالِحِيْنَ
دَرَجَةً بِبَلَاءٍ فَبَلِّغْنِيْهَا بِالعَافِيَةِ

Allāhumma in kunta ballaghta aḥadan min ʿibādika
al-ṣāliḥīna darajatan bi-balāʾin fa-ballighnīhā bil-ʿāfiyah

O Allah, if You have granted any righteous servant of
Yours a station because of a trial they faced, then grant
it to me while sparing me that trial.

❦

When we deal with a hardship, we often ask ourselves the reason we are being subjected to that hardship. We are told it is because of the great reward that can come as a result of it, if we internalize and act upon it in the way that the Prophet *(peace be upon him)* taught us to act in a time of hardship. You hear lessons of Allah *(glorified and exalted is He)* showering people who have been through hardship and trials with the mercy that He does, and you start to wonder if this is the only way one can gain the pleasure of Allah *(glorified and exalted is He)*; as in the hadith of the Prophet *(peace be upon him)* that Allah tests those whom He loves.

So can we only attain the love of Allah through severe trials and tests? This is the sentiment that would be present in the Hereafter, when the Prophet *(peace be upon him)* said, 'When *ahl al-ʿāfiyah (people who were spared from hardship)* see *ahl al-balāʾ (people who were tested)* being rewarded by Allah in the Hereafter, they would wish to be returned to the world so that they would cut their skins'. So Allah *(glorified and exalted is He)* is the One who consoles and comforts, and Allah is the One who allots this immense reward for the struggles of the righteous. Hence the question: is there any way for us to attain a high position with Allah *(glorified and exalted is He)* without going through

Be graceful when Allah tests you because it might be the case that we can only reach that station of Allah's pleasure by going through that trial and test.

severe hardship? And how do we reconcile that notion with the *du'ā'* in the Qur'an:

> 'O Allah! We ask you the best of this life and the best of the Hereafter and protect us from the Fire of Hell.' (al-Baqarah 2:201)

In a similar vein, Salam ibn Muti' *(may Allah be pleased with him)* was heard making this *du'ā'*: 'O Allah, if you have granted any righteous servant of Yours a station because of a trial they faced, then grant it to me while sparing me that trial.' Allah is capable of giving the best of this life and the best of the next, so don't ask Allah for trials and tests but still seek reward. Be graceful when Allah tests you because it might be the case that we can only reach that station of Allah's pleasure by going through that trial and test. At the same time, when asking Allah know that you are asking from a merciful Lord, a capable Lord, so ask the best from Him.

May Allah *(glorified and exalted is He)* grant us the best of this life and the best of the Hereafter and protect us from the punishment of Hell. May He grant us the highest station of seekers, and the highest station of the patient, and the highest station of the grateful without putting us through trials that could potentially compromise that patience and allow us to lose out on that reward. *Āmīn.*

❧ 14 ❧

My Evil

— VS —

His Good

اللَّهُمَّ لَا تَحْرِمْنِي خَيْرَ مَا عِنْدَكَ لِشَرِّ مَا عِنْدِي

*Allāhumma lā-taḥrimnī khayra mā-ʿindaka
li-sharri mā-ʿindī*

**O Allah, do not forbid me from
the good You have, for the evil I have.**

———— ✦ ————

When you are looking at the prayers of the pious
you expect to find the names of well-known
people from the Salaf, but sometimes the most pious
people go unknown in this world and in fact can impress
those who are known for their piety. This is a particular

incident that took place in the lifetime of one of the greatest scholars of all time, Imam Sufyan al-Thawri *(may Allah be pleased with him)*. He was sitting in the *masjid* one day between the prayers, supplicating to Allah and reciting the remembrances of Allah *(glorified and exalted is He)*, when he saw a man who was calling upon Him. This man made a *duʿāʾ* that 'stuck with me for the rest of my life'. He said that the man called out to Allah *(glorified and exalted is He)* and said: 'O Allah do not forbid me from the good you have, for the evil I have.'

Sufyan recalls that this unknown man's *duʿāʾ* 'was more beautiful than I had known and that I had been making in my own personal life'. There is a lot of power to this *duʿāʾ* and it fits with the Prophetic equation once again that as you are calling upon Allah *(glorified and exalted is He)* asking for something, then understand that the more good that He has descended upon us, the more that our evil ascends towards Him, and the more that our ingratitude in our sins ascend towards Him. Once again this is the acknowledgement from the Prophet *(peace be upon him)* in the *duʿāʾ* of *Sayyid al-Istighfar (the master prayer for seeking forgiveness)*:

'I fully admit the good that You have given me, the blessings that You have bestowed upon me and I admit my sins that I have ascended to You.'

This is one of those *duʿāʾ*s that we can all make; O Allah, we depend fully on Your mercy, so forgive us and show mercy upon us and do not let our sins or our shortcomings disqualify us from that mercy in this life or the next. *Āmīn.*

I fully admit the good that You have given me, the blessings that You have bestowed upon me and I admit my sins that I have ascended to You.

❧ 15 ❧

The Prayer
of a Tree

اللَّهُمَّ اكْتُبْ لِي بِهَا عِنْدَكَ أَجراً، وَضَعْ عَنِّي بِهَا وِزْراً، وَاجْعَلْهَا لِي عِندَكَ ذُخْراً، وَتَقَبَّلْهَا مِنِّي كَمَا تَقَبَّلْتَهَا مِنْ عَبْدِكَ دَاوُدَ عَلَيْهِ الصَّلَاةُ وَالسَّلَامُ

Allāhumma uktub lī bihā ʿindaka ajran, wa-ḍaʿ ʿannī bihā wizran, wa-jʿalhā lī ʿindaka dhukhran, wa-taqabbalhā minnī kamā taqabbaltahā min ʿabdika Dawūda ʿalahi al-ṣalātu wal-salām

O Allah, write for me a reward with You because of it (the prostration), and remove from me a sin because of it, and stow it for me as a treasure with You, and accept it from me as You have accepted it from Your servant David (Dawud), upon him be blessings and peace.

We have looked at the prayers of people that aren't entirely heroes or villains, of many of the Companions and the righteous predecessors, of scholars, and even unknown people who were able to benefit some of those great scholars. But what about the *du‘ā'* of a tree? This is a hadith, an authentic one from at-Tirmidhi, of a man who had a dream of a tree making *du‘ā'* and he conveyed this dream to the Prophet *(peace be upon him)*.

The Prophet *(peace be upon him)* used to ask the Companions, 'who amongst you saw a dream last night that we could benefit from?' A man stood up and said to the Prophet *(peace be upon him)*, 'O Messenger of Allah! Last night I had a dream, a very strange dream'. He said, 'while I was sleeping, it was as if I was praying behind a tree. It was a tree which was basically my Imam *(and dreams can obviously have different symbols and different meanings)*. I was praying and there was a tree in front of me. I prostrated and then the tree prostrated as well, and then I heard the tree make *du‘ā'*. The tree said: "O Allah, write for me a reward with You because of it *(the prostration)* and remove from me a sin because of it, and accept it from me as You accepted it from Your servant David, upon him be blessings and peace."'

The tree is making *du'ā'*, and obviously it's not an actual tree but the man is learning a prayer and everything glorifies Allah *(glorified and exalted is He)*. The Prophet *(peace be upon him)* loved this narration so much, and saw it as a form of divine wisdom and pleasure, that he made *sujūd* and made the same *du'ā'*, which teaches us many lessons. One of the things we learn is that as you are making *sujūd*, as you are prostrating, recognize that the most beloved station, the most beloved position that you are in with Allah *(glorified and exalted is He)* is prostration. This is a lesson that Sufyan ibn 'Uyaynah *(may Allah be pleased with him)* mentioned: only human beings can make a perfect *sujūd*. Our bodies are created to pray, to prostrate. All of our limbs touch the ground the way that they do, with our foreheads on the ground calling upon Allah in prayer and humility, and there is nothing more beloved to Allah than that. The Prophet *(peace be upon him)* mentioned that you are closest to Allah in your prostration. So when you go into prostration, that's the time to make special prayer, especially in the *nawafil (voluntary prayers)*.

May Allah *(glorified and exalted is He)* accept our prayers and our prostrations. May He allow that humility to be conveyed in our prostration to Him in our prayer as well as in obedience to His commands. *Āmīn*.

You are closest to Allah in your prostration. So when you go into prostration, that's the time to make special prayer.

❧ 16 ❧

A House on Fire

بِسْمِ اللهِ الَّذِي لَا يَضُرُّ مَعَ اسْمِهِ شَيْءٌ فِي الْأَرْضِ
وَلَا فِي السَّمَاءِ وَهُوَ السَّمِيعُ الْعَلِيمُ

*Bismi Allahi al-ladhī lā-yaḍurru maʿa ismihī
shay'un fī al-arḍi wa-lā fī al-samā'i wa-huwa
al-samīʿu al-ʿalīmu*

**In the name of Allah; with His name, nothing
whatsoever on earth or heaven can inflict any harm;
He is All-Hearing and All-Knowing.**

---- ✦ ----

This particular incident doesn't have words to
memorize as much as it is a lesson in how much you
believe in your *duʿā'*. Often, when you see people making
an exquisite supplication, they have already defeated the
purpose of the supplication because they don't believe in

what they're saying. Ibn Qayyim *(may Allah be pleased with him)* said that if you really have tawakkul, trust in Allah, the way He deserves to be trusted, then you can move mountains.

An incident was narrated by Abū Mūsā al-Ash'ari *(may Allah be pleased with him)* that he says he witnessed in Basra *(Iraq)*. He saw an entire neighbourhood catch fire. As that happened, people went to the marketplace to inform the residents of the neighbourhood to get to their homes as quickly as possible and to try to do something about it. He said, 'we came across a man whose house was in that neighbourhood and told him to get to his home in a hurry. The man responded, "I'm not worried about my home burning down".' Upon asking why he wasn't worried the man said, 'I've taken an oath upon my Lord that it will not burn down', meaning the man was so confident and so sincere in his *du'ā'* that Allah *(glorified and exalted is He)* would not let the house burn down. Eventually, after all of the neighbourhood had burned and the smoke cleared, all the homes were harmed apart from the home of this man.

Abū Mūsā *(may Allah be pleased with him)* said, 'I heard the Messenger of Allah say that in my nation there are men with bare heads and unkempt clothing', meaning there are people that are very simple and looked down upon in society; people that have nothing to show for themselves in terms of wealth and position. But for those people, if they swear upon their Lord, Allah *(glorified and exalted is He)* would fulfil their oaths. There is another Hadith where the Prophet *(peace be upon him)* said there are people that might be unkempt and turned away by others, but if that person were to take an oath upon God, Allah will honour that oath.

This is a very powerful example of the idea that Allah is accessible to the most simple of people, to those with nothing who might be looked down upon by society. A person might have no power in this world, in the sense that they have no respect, no financial status—especially in a feudal society—no class that would protect them or they belong to some sort of oppressed minority—they are disadvantaged and downtrodden by all—but that person has access to the Most Powerful, the One who is *al-Qādir* and *al-Muqtadir (The Omnipotent)*. If they truly believe in their *du'ā'* and they ask Allah *(glorified and exalted is He)* most sincerely, Allah will most certainly honour their prayers.

There is one more narration that I would like to share with you, which happened to Abū Dardā' *(may Allah be pleased with him)* the great scholar and mufti of the Companions. His neighborhood burned down, like that of the man in Basra, and his home was also not destroyed. The reason he gave for the protection of his home was that he made a supplication to his Lord that the Prophet *(peace be upon him)* taught him: 'In the name of Allah; with His name, nothing whatsoever on earth or heaven can inflict any harm; He is All-Hearing and All-Knowing'. He said, 'The Prophet *(peace be upon him)* taught us to say this *duʿā'* three times every morning and three times in the evening'.

May Allah *(glorified and exalted is He)* allow us to truly believe in our *duʿā'* and to show us the power of our supplication through His power. Allow us to develop that meaningful trust that translates into miracles in this world and into salvation in the Hereafter. *Āmīn.*

His Prayer Amazed the Prophet ﷺ

يَا مَنْ لَا تَرَاهُ العُيُوْنُ، وَلَا تُخَالِطُهُ الظُّنُوْنُ، وَلَا يَصِفُهُ الوَاصِفُوْنَ، وَلَا تُغَيِّرُهُ الحَوَادِثُ، وَلَا يَخْشَى الدَّوَائِرَ، يَعْلَمُ مَثَاقِيْلَ الجِبَالِ، وَمَكَايِيْلَ البِحَارِ، وَعَدَدَ قَطْرِ الأَمْطَارِ، وَعَدَدَ وَرَقِ الأَشْجَارِ، وَعَدَدَ مَا أَظْلَمَ عَلَيْهِ اللَّيْلُ وَأَشْرَقَ عَلَيْهِ النَّهَارُ، وَلَا تُوَارِيْ مِنْهُ سَمَاءٌ سَمَاءً، وَلَا أَرْضٌ أَرْضاً، وَلَا بَحْرٌ مَا فِي قَعْرِهِ، وَلَا جَبَلٌ مَا فِي وَعْرِهِ، اجْعَلْ خَيْرَ عُمْرِي آخِرَهُ، وَخَيْرَ عَمَلِي خَوَاتِيْمَهُ، وَخَيْرَ أَيَّامِي يَوْمَ أَلقَاكَ فِيْهِ

Yā-man lā-tarāhu al-ʿuyūnu wa-lā tukhāliṭuhu
al-ẓunūnu wa-lā yaṣifuhu al-wāṣifūna wa-lā tughayyiruhu
al-ḥawādithu, wa-lā yakhshā al-dawāʾira, yaʿlamu
mathāqīla al-jibāli, wa-makāyīla al-biḥāri wa-ʿadada
qaṭri al-amṭāri, wa-ʿadada waraqi al-ashjāri, wa-ʿadada
mā-aẓlama ʿalayhi al-laylu wa-ashraqa ʿalayhi al-nahāru,
wa-lā tuwārī minhu samāʾun samāʾan, wa-lā arḍun
arḍan, wa-lā baḥrun mā-fī qaʿrihi, wa-lā jabalun mā-fī
waʿrihi, ijʿal khayra ʿumrī ākhirahu wa-khayra ʿamalī
khawātimahu, wa-khayra ayyāmī yawma alqāka fīh

Oh, He whom the eyes do not see, nor can be mixed
with doubt, nor can be described by any who describe,
nor is changed by any events, nor fears any oppressor
or person of perceived power; who knows the weights
of the mountains, the measurements of the seas,
the number of raindrops, the number of leaves on
trees, and the number of whatever is shrouded in the
darkness of night and brightened by the light of day,
for whom no heaven or earth is concealed, nor a
sea in its depths, nor a mountain in its ruggedness!
Make the best of my life the end of it, the best of
my deeds the last of them, and the best of
my days the Day I meet You.

This is a very special narration, similar to when the Prophet *(peace be upon him)* heard the *du'ā'* of 'Abdullah ibn Mas'ūd *(may Allah be pleased with him)*. He is walking by a man in a *masjid* and overhears the prayer of a pious man, an unknown Bedouin, calling upon Allah *(glorified and exalted is He)*. The Prophet *(peace be upon him)* does not know this man but his *du'ā'* amazes him. The Prophet *(peace be upon him)* is connected to his Lord closer than anyone else, so he senses that connection when he hears it from other people and he appreciates the genuine relationship that someone might have with Allah *(glorified and exalted is He)*. Even if the pious don't call upon Him in the most perfect of ways, they call upon Him knowing how capable He is.

In the statement preceding his *du'ā'*, the man encompasses all of the elements of nature—the mountains, the seas, the rain, and the trees—but he also understands that there are some things that are not perceived in terms of nature, and he brings all of creation into his *du'ā'*. This teaches us that the praise of our Lord can never be exaggerated, so you praise and you praise and you praise. Then he makes his *du'ā'*, and it sounds familiar: 'Make the best of my life the end of it, the best of my deeds the last of them, and the best of my days the Day I meet You.' It's almost verbatim of the *du'ā'* made by Abū Bakr al-Ṣiddīq *(may Allah be pleased with him)*, the first *du'ā'* discussed in this book.

Amazed by the Bedouin's *du'ā'*, the Prophet *(peace be upon him)* appoints a man to stay with him and to wait for him to finish his prayers, and to inform the Prophet *(peace be upon him)* when he is done. When the Bedouin has finished, the Prophet *(peace be upon him)* comes over to him and asks the man who he is and where he's from. The Bedouin tells the Prophet *(peace be upon him)* that he's just a man from Banū 'Amr *(an Arabian tribe in Quba', on the outskirts of Madinah)* and the Prophet *(peace be upon him)* gives him a gift. The Prophet *(peace be upon him)* asks, 'do you know why I'm giving you this gift?' He continues, 'maybe we're related'. The Prophet *(peace be upon him)* knows, he says, because of the beauty of the Bedouin's praise of Allah *(glorified and exalted is He)*. Subhan Allah. An individual does not have to be a poet to praise Allah, you'd be surprised how poetic you can be when you are sincere.

May Allah *(glorified and exalted is He)*, the Creator of the heavens and the earth, He who knows the weights of the mountains and the measurements of the seas, forgive us and make the best of our lives the end of them and the best of our deeds the last of them, and the best of our days the Day that we meet Him. *Āmīn.*

A Reminder of My Illness

أَذْهِبِ البَأْسَ رَبَّ النَّاسِ، وَاشْفِ أَنْتَ الشَّافِي، لَا شِفَاءَ
إِلَّا شِفَاؤُكَ شِفَاءً لَا يُغَادِرُ سَقَماً

Adhhibi al-ba'sa rabba al-nāsi, wa'shfi anta al-shāfī
lā-shifā'a illā shifā'uka shifā'an lā-yughādiru saqaman

Remove the illness O Sustainer of Mankind. Cure the disease, for You are the One Who cures, there is no cure except Your cure. Grant me a cure that leaves no illness.

———— ✦ ————

Uways al-Qarni *(may Allah be pleased with him)* was a man that the Prophet *(peace be upon him)* spoke about but never met. He told his Companions that if they ever met this man, because of his closeness to

Allah *(glorified and exalted is He)* they should ask him
to ask Allah to seek forgiveness for them, and he gave a
description of Uways. The Prophet *(peace be upon him)*
described his deeds in two ways: He said that Uways
had leprosy and he asked Allah *(glorified and exalted is
He)* to cure him from the leprosy except for a piece the
size of a coin, a dirham. Uways was also a man who was
very generous or would show extreme obedience to his
mother, and because of the obedience to his mother,
Allah *(glorified and exalted is He)* honoured him.

Every year that people came for Hajj, ʿUmar ibn
Khaṭṭāb *(may Allah be pleased with him)* would ask
caravans, particularly from Yemen, if Uways was among
them. Eventually ʿUmar found him, and he started to
question Uways about his description, where he was
from, his tribe, and if he was the man that the Prophet
(peace be upon him) spoke about. After establishing
and understanding who this man was, and that he
was indeed the Uways the Prophet referred to, ʿUmar
requested him to seek forgiveness from Allah *(glorified
and exalted is He)* for him.

Usually in this narration, we focus on the part of the
mother, from the fact that the greatest way to come
closer to Allah is to honour your parents. Indeed, Ibn
ʿAbbās *(may Allah be pleased with him)* says he knew of

no other action that brings one closer to Allah than the honouring of one's mother. However, in this instance we will focus on the prior sentence, which isn't usually discussed in any explanation of the hadith and in the context of *du'ā'*. Uways *(may Allah be pleased with him)* suffered from leprosy and he asked Allah to cure him from his leprosy but to leave a dirham-size piece of leprosy on him. Why do you think he would do that? He did that because it was a reminder of the pain that he had suffered and the need to always be grateful to Allah *(glorified and exalted is He)* to have cured him.

That's a very powerful example of character. Many times we call upon Allah *(glorified and exalted is He)* in our desperation and ask Him to remove a hardship from us. We make promises to Allah *(glorified and exalted is He)* if He removes the hardship, but as soon as He does so we become heedless once again and we forget not only the blessings of the removal of the hardship but also the promises that we made. Hence this is an extraordinary lesson; when you are calling upon Allah *(glorified and exalted is He)*, asking for Him to relieve you of a hardship, ask also for a reminder of the lesson of that hardship, because the closest you are to Allah is often at your deepest moments of vulnerability and hardship, and you don't want that to leave you. Often, when Allah *(glorified and exalted is He)* takes something away from you, He gives you something better, and the greatest thing that Allah can give you in exchange for something you lose in this world is Himself. That's what Uways al-Qarni gained from his hardship, that deep relationship with Allah which he never wanted to forget, even as he wanted to be cured from his leprosy.

May Allah *(glorified and exalted is He)* grant us humility and relieve us of our hardships, but do not allow us to forget the lessons that we learned from them, and may He grant us the best of this world and the Hereafter. *Āmīn.*

❧ 19 ❧

Make Me Better

اللَّهُمَّ اجْعَلْنِي خَيْرًا مِمَّا يَظُنُّونَ وَاغْفِرْ لِي
مَا لَا يَعْلَمُونَ وَلَا تُؤَاخِذْنِي بِمَا يَقُولُون

*Allāhumma ijʿalnī khayran mimmā yaẓunnūna waghfir
lī mā-lā yaʿlamūna wa-lā tuʾākhidhnī bimā yaqūlūna*

**O Allah, make me better than how they think of me, and
forgive me for what they do not know about me, and do
not take me to account for what they say about me.**

❖

Other people may think of us things that are not
true and one of the most feared thoughts for
those that are often glorified, or someone who is given
undue praise, is that because they don't meet that praise
when they meet Allah (*glorified and exalted is He*) they
are held accountable for those things other people say

of them of good. The Prophet *(peace be upon him)* told us of this frightening scenario, that when someone is buried and people start to eulogize about them and say good things, the angels poke at that person and ask them if they were really as they say they were? Was that person really as the people describe them?

This is not something that just applies to the great scholar, or to the perceived great scholar or the preacher. It applies to every person who was deemed righteous in the public eye. Just as we hate slander, we hate destructive praise, because it can put us in a state of hypocrisy *(may Allah protect us)*. Abū Bakr *(may Allah be pleased with him)* was very aware of that and he used to make it a point to hide his good deeds. Often, other Companions would find Abū Bakr secretly doing good deeds; imagine how many deeds Abū Bakr *(may Allah be pleased with him)* did that we were never aware of, that the books never encompassed, and what he teaches us in this *duʿāʾ* is essential to every person in the public eye.

If you look at the first part of this *duʿāʾ*, the word that is used is *ẓann* because people might think something of Abū Bakr that is untrue and he does not think he is as good as others think he is. Then Abū Bakr asks, 'forgive me for what they don't know about me', meaning that he may have shortcomings and sins of which people are unaware. He even uses different language: 'Forgive me for that which they don't know about me that I know about myself,' and he continues, 'and do not hold me accountable for the things they say about me.' If anything, we want Allah to bring about good testimony from people on the Day of Judgement, but we want to make sure it is character testimony that means something. The *shahādah,* the witnessing of the people on this earth, should mean something of good, and we want to make sure that we're actually living up to that and it was not all a false portrayal.

Ibn al-Jawzi *(may Allah be pleased with him),* whose prayer we have already covered, said that if people are impressed with you, don't think that they're impressed by you. They're impressed by the beauty of Allah's cover *(hijāb)* placed over your sins; it's not really you, it's the veil that Allah has provided. You need to be self-aware of that so that you can continue to work on those things and not allow for destructive praise to sedate you or paralyze you from actually living up to the best of yourself.

May Allah *(glorified and exalted is He)* make us better than people think of us, may He forgive us for things people don't know of us, and may He not hold us accountable for the things that they say about us. *Āmīn.*

The shahādah, the witnessing of the people on this earth, should mean something of good, and we want to make sure that we're actually living up to that and it was not all a false portrayal.

Don't Ask Allah for Patience

عَنْ مُعَاذِ بْنِ جَبَلٍ، قَالَ سَمِعَ النَّبِيُّ صَلَّى اللهُ عَلَيْهِ وَسَلَّمَ رَجُلاً يَدْعُو يَقُولُ اللَّهُمَّ إِنِّي أَسْأَلُكَ تَمَامَ النِّعْمَةِ. فَقَالَ: أَيُّ شَيْءٍ تَمَامُ النِّعْمَةِ. قَالَ دَعْوَةٌ دَعَوْتُ بِهَا أَرْجُو بِهَا الْخَيْرَ. قَالَ: فَإِنَّ مِنْ تَمَامِ النِّعْمَةِ دُخُولَ الْجَنَّةِ وَالْفَوْزَ مِنَ النَّارِ. وَسَمِعَ رَجُلاً وَهُوَ يَقُولُ يَا ذَا الْجَلاَلِ وَالإِكْرَام فَقَالَ: قَدِ اسْتُجِيبَ لَكَ فَسَلْ. وَسَمِعَ النَّبِيُّ صَلَّى اللهُ عَلَيْهِ وَسَلَّمَ رَجُلاً وَهُوَ يَقُولُ اللَّهُمَّ إِنِّي أَسْأَلُكَ الصَّبْرَ. فَقَالَ: سَأَلْتَ اللهَ الْبَلاَءَ فَسَلْهُ الْعَافِيَةَ

*'An Mu'ādhin ibni jabalin qāla: sami'a al-nabiyyu
ṣalla Allāhu 'alayhi wa-sallam rajulan yad'ū yaqūlu:
Allāhumma innī as'ulaka tamāma al-ni'mati, faqāla:
ayyu shay'in tamāmu al-ni'mati? Qāla: da'watun
da'awtu bihā arju bihā al-khayra. Qāla: fa'inna min
tamāmi al-ni'mati dukhūla al-jannati wal-fawza mina
al-nāri. Wa-sami'a rajulan wa-huwa yaqūlu: yā dha
al-jalāli wal-ikrāmi, faqāla: qad uṣtujība laka fasal. Wa-
sami'a al-nabiyyu ṣalla Allāhu 'alayhi wa-sallam rajulan
wa-huwa yaqūlu: Allāhumma innī as'ulaka al-ṣabra,
faqāla: sa'alta Allaha al-balā'a fasalhu al-'āfiyah*

*Mu'adh ibn Jabal narrated that the Prophet (peace
and blessings of Allah be upon him) heard a man
supplicating, saying: 'O Allah! Verily, I ask You for the
bounty's completion.' So he said: 'What is the bounty's
completion?' The man replied: 'A supplication that
I made, that I hope for good by it.' He said: 'Indeed, part
of the bounty's completion is the entrance into Paradise,
and salvation from the Fire.' And he heard a man while
he was saying: 'O Possessor of Majesty and Honour.'
So he said: 'You have been responded to, so ask.' And
the Prophet (peace and blessings of Allah be upon him)
heard a man while he was saying: 'O Allah, indeed,
I ask You for patience.' He said: 'You have asked Allah
for hardship, instead ask him for ease.'*

I magine the Prophet *(peace be upon him)* walking around the *masjid,* monitoring people's *du'ā's* and commenting on the way that they are supplicating to Allah *(glorified and exalted is He).* Like a Qur'an teacher walks around the room and checks up on people as they are reciting their Qur'an, making sure that they're reciting it properly, so the Prophet *(peace be upon him)* was making sure that worshippers were supplicating properly. This is a narration from Mu'adh ibn Jabal *(may Allah be pleased with him)* where the Prophet *(peace be upon him)* is commenting on the *du'ā's* of other people, and it is a great lesson for us into the 'dos and don'ts' of the *du'ā'.*

The first man the Prophet *(peace be upon him)* overheard was asking Allah *(glorified and exalted is He)* for, 'the bounty's completion'. When the Prophet *(peace be upon him)* asked what he meant by that, the man replied it was a supplication that made him feel good. So the Prophet *(peace be upon him)* confirmed to him that the completion of the bounty means salvation, entering into Paradise and protection from Hellfire, but he made sure to tell the man that by making his *du'ā',* he must make sure that he intends that. The Prophet *(peace be upon him)* then passed another man, who was addressing Allah *(glorified and exalted is He)* as 'Possessor of Majesty and Honour'. This is one of the ways that the Prophet *(peace be upon him)* himself used to call upon Allah, so he spoke to the man and said, 'You have been responded to, so ask!' Here the Prophet *(peace be upon him)* is suggesting that the man has addressed Allah *(glorified and exalted is He)* as the Prophet had also addressed Him and by God's Messenger responding to the man then he should go ahead and make *duʿāʾ*, his supplication.

Finally, the Prophet *(peace be upon him)* heard a third man making a *duʿāʾ*, and he was asking: 'O Allah, indeed, I ask You for patience'. The question here is, can someone ask Allah for patience, is it a good thing? In reply, the Prophet *(peace be upon him)* told the man, 'you have asked Allah for hardships, instead ask Him for ease'. How do we reconcile this? Don't we all want to be *aṣ-ṣābirūn (the patient, who will get their reward in full without any reckoning)?* Didn't the Prophet *(peace be upon him)* say that Allah *(glorified and exalted is He)* has never given to any of His servants a gift more expansive and more comprehensive than *ṣabr (patience)?* So why did the Prophet *(peace be upon him)* tell the man not to ask Allah for patience and ask Him for ease *(ʿāfiyah)* instead?

In fact, the Prophet *(peace be upon him)* was referring to a specific context. It's not about asking Allah *(glorified and exalted is He)* for patience, which is a great quality to have, or to be in the station of the patient, which is a great station to be in, but in this situation, when you're going through a hardship, instead of asking Him for patience to go through that hardship, ask Allah to remove that hardship from you and demonstrate patience in your very being. Instead of asking Allah *(glorified and exalted is He)* with a spirit of uncertainty and expectation of hardship and trial, ask Him with the expectation of good and ease. If trial does come to you, accept that trial as good and as a form of ease in its full context. Hence the Prophet *(peace be upon him)* did not approve of the man making his *duʿāʾ* for patience, instead he taught us to ask for *ʿĀfiyah,* to ask Allah *(glorified and exalted is He)* to be spared and to take with grace and patience whatever comes our way.

May Allah *(glorified and exalted is He)* grant us the quality of *ṣabr* and grant us the station of *aṣ-ṣābirūn.* May He grant us *ʿĀfiyah,* pardon and forgiveness and allow us to be spared in this life, and grant us the best in this life and the next. *Āmīn.*

Instead of asking Allah for patience to go through a hardship, ask Him to remove that hardship from you and demonstrate patience in your very being.

❧ 21 ❧

Death After Fajr

اللَّهُمَّ اجْعَلْ خَاتِمَةَ عَمَلِي صَلَاةَ الفَجْرِ

Allāhumma ij'al khātimata 'amalī ṣalāta al-fajri

**O Allah! Make my last deed in this life
the performance of Fajr prayer.**

❖

There is a tendency in the prayers of the pious of asking Allah *(glorified and exalted is He)* for a good ending, because the Prophet *(peace be upon him)* himself taught us to ask Allah for a good ending. In life, you have high points and low points, and you don't want Allah to send the Angel of Death to you when you are at a low point. There are many ways of asking Allah for a good ending, and anyone who has been around dying righteous people may have noticed that in the last days of their lives it was almost as if they had been informed, that they knew they were going to die. That's something you feel, Subhan Allah, it's not something that could be explained. It's not that there is some sort of explicit communication to people, but there is a feeling and that's something that was narrated on behalf of many of the Salaf, the pious predecessors.

This particular *duʿāʾ*, of a man who knew that his time had come and who felt that closeness—similar to Hudhayfah ibn al-Yaman *(may Allah be pleased with him)*, is a very simple *duʿāʾ*. One night, ʿAbdullah ibn Abi Sarh *(may Allah be pleased with him)* was praying his night prayer and he was so joyful in that *qiyam* that he asked Allah *(glorified and exalted is He)* directly that this Fajr be his last deed. He didn't say *this* salat-al-Fajr, he said salat al-Fajr, meaning the morning prayer, be the last of his deeds. Since he had a routine of praying at night, he felt that closeness to Allah, and for the ones who stand and pray at night Fajr is not the beginning of the day as much as it is the conclusion of the night. So he finished his qiyam, made his wudu' and prayed his Fajr and died at the conclusion of salat al-Fajr. Subhan Allah.

It was not a death on a battlefield, nor a stabbing or something overdramatic. It was a simple recognition that there are some people who feel that moment and they ask Allah *(glorified and exalted is He)* for that last good ending.

He was praying his night prayer and he was so joyful in that qiyam that he asked Allah directly that this Fajr be his last deed.

'Urwah *(may Allah be pleased with him)* made *du'ā'* to Allah *(glorified and exalted is He)* in *sujūd* to die in prostration, and it's a good thing to ask Allah that you die in prayer, or that you meet Allah in prayer or that the last of your deeds be prayers. So we ask Allah *(glorified and exalted is He)* to take us back in the state that's most beloved to Him, at a time that's most beloved to Him and in a state of humility that's beloved to Him.

May Allah *(glorified and exalted is He)* give us lives that are pleasing to Him and let our death come to us at the most pleasing times of our lives and again make the best of our days be the Day that we meet Him. *Āmīn.*

22

Your Perfect Light

تَمَّ نُورُكَ فَهَدَيْتَ فَلَكَ الْحَمْدُ. عَظُمَ حِلْمُكَ فَعَفَوْتَ
فَلَكَ الْحَمْدُ. وَبَسَطْتَ يَدَكَ فَأَعْطَيْتَ فَلَكَ الْحَمْدُ.
رَبَّنَا وَجْهُكَ أَكْرَمُ الْوُجُوهِ ، وَجَاهُكَ خَيْرُ الْجَاهِ،
وَعَطِيَّتُكَ أَفْضَلُ الْعَطِيَّةِ وَأَهْنَأُهَا. تُطَاعُ رَبَّنَا
فَتَشْكُرُ ، وَتُعْصَى رَبَّنَا فَتَغْفِرُ لِمَنْ شِئْتَ. تُجِيبُ
الْمُضْطَرَّ ، وَتَكْشِفُ الضُّرَّ ، وَتَشْفِي السَّقِيمَ ،
وَتُنْجِي مِنَ الْكَرْبِ ، وَتَقْبَلُ التَّوْبَةَ ، وَتَغْفِرُ الذُّنُوبَ ،
لَا يَجْزِي بِآلَائِكَ وَلَا يُحْصِي نَعْمَاءَكَ قَوْلُ قَائِلٍ

*Tamma nūruka fa-hadayta fa-laka al-ḥamdu. ʿAẓuma
ḥilmuka fa-ʿafawta fa-laka al-ḥamdu. Wa-basatta
yadaka fa-aʿṭayta fa-laka al-ḥamdu. Rabbanā wajhuka
akramu al-wujūhi wa-jāhuka khayru al-jāhi
wa-ʿaṭiyyatuka afḍalu al-ʿaṭiyyati wa-ahnaʾuhā.
Tuṭāʿu rabbanā fa-tashkuru wa-tuṣā rabbanā fataghfiru
liman shiʾt. Tujību al-muḍtarra wa-takshifu al-ḍurra
wa-tashfi al-saqīma wa-tunjī mina al-karbi wa-taqbalu
al-tawbata wa-taghfiru al-dhunūba, lā-yajzī bi-ālāʾika
wa-lā yuḥṣī naʿmāʾaka qawlu qāʾilin*

**Your light was complete, so You guided; all praise is
to You. Your forbearance was great, so You forgave;
all praise is to You. You held out Your Hand, so
You gave; all praise is to You. Our Lord, Your face
is the noblest of faces, Your prestige is the greatest
prestige, and Your gifts are the best of gifts and the
most wonderful. Our Lord, You are obeyed and You
show appreciation. You are disobeyed, O Lord, yet
You pardon whomever you wish. You respond to one
in hardship and You remove harm. You heal the sick.
You deliver from difficulty. You accept repentance.
You forgive sins. The word of no one can compensate
for Your bounties, nor count the praises You deserve.**

✦

There are some Companions of the Prophet *(peace be upon him)* who were so poetic with everything that they said and everything that they did. One of those is ʿAli ibn Abi Talib *(may Allah be pleased with him)*, the cousin and son-in-law of the Prophet *(peace be upon him)*, and one of the first believers. ʿAli was near and dear to the Prophet *(peace be upon him)* and he resembled him in many different ways.

This *duʿāʾ* is a narration of the *qiyām duʿāʾ*, the nightly prayer of ʿAli *(may Allah be pleased with him)* that he would stand and recite. It's a long but poetic *duʿāʾ*, and at the end of it all ʿAli knows that no matter how much you praise Allah *(glorified and exalted is He)*, you will never be able to fully encompass the praise and the gratitude that He is due. As long as you call upon Allah and show gratitude and praise Him for His creation, praise Him for His mercy, praise Him for His bounties, praise Him for His forgiveness, Allah will not disappoint. No amount of praise can truly encompass the praise that He is due, because His mercy and benevolence exceeds all the praise that we could ever express.

May Allah *(glorified and exalted is He)* allow us to praise Him as beautifully as ʿAli *(may Allah be pleased with him)*, this beautiful servant of His, and to not be let down and to be guaranteed Paradise as 'Ali was guaranteed Paradise. *Āmīn*.

❦ 23 ❦

My Sincerity to Your Creation

اللَّهُمَّ إِنِّي نَصَحْتُ لِخَلْقِكَ ظَاهِراً وَغَشَشْتُ نَفْسِي
بَاطِناً، فَهَبْ لِي غِشِّي لِنَفْسِي لِنُصْحِي لِخَلْقِكَ

*Allāhumma innī naṣaḥtu li-khalqika ẓāhiran
wa-ghashashtu nafsī bāṭinan, fa-hab lī ghisshī
li-nafsī li-nuṣḥī li-khalqika*

**O Allah, I was sincere to Your creation in public but
cheated myself in private. Please excuse my disgrace
because of my sincerity to Your creation.**

———————— ✦ ————————

Here we have a group of people surrounding an elderly scholar, Yusuf ibn al-Husayn *(may Allah be pleased with him)*, and someone asks of him, 'O Father of Ya'qūb *(his son's name was Ya'qūb, as men used to love to name their children after the prophets)*, share with us one of these *du'ā's.*' Often, these personal supplications contain deep lessons, so Yusuf thought for a while and then said, 'O Allah, I was sincere to Your creation in public but I cheated myself in private. Please excuse my private disgrace because of my sincerity to Your creation.' After sharing this *du'ā'*, he cried and passed away, so this *du'ā'* has a deep meaning that is not found in any other supplication in this series.

Often, you will find someone with empathy or sincerity to the creation of Allah *(glorified and exalted is He)* but in the process of being sincere to the creation of Allah, they lose sincerity with Him. They lose those private moments of devotion and they excuse themselves from doing those things because of the great deeds they do in public. That's why you'll find that some of the greatest people in history had the greatest flaws. It's very easy to be fooled into thinking that because someone is doing great things for everyone else they don't have to worry about themselves in private; they might think, 'I can excuse a little bit of excess in private'. Here we have this great scholar, Yusuf ibn al-Husayn *(may Allah be pleased with him)*, who is calling upon Allah *(glorified and exalted is He)* with full acknowledgement, and he says: I was sincere to Your creation in public but I was disgraceful in private. He didn't harm anybody but he did harm himself, so Yusuf asks Allah *(glorified and exalted is He)* for forgiveness for that private disgrace because of his sincerity to His creation. The *duʿā'* contains an acknowledgement that Yusuf fell short in private, but he wants to be forgiven for that, and Allah knows whether his private life actually had anything that was deeply flawed or it was simply the high standard to which he held himself.

May Allah *(glorified and exalted is He)* forgive us for the sins that we do in private that harm ourselves because of the good that we do for His creation, and that is certainly beloved to Allah *(glorified and exalted is He)*. May Allah rectify our private and our public lives in a way that is most pleasing to Him. *Āmīn*.

Often, you will find someone with empathy or sincerity to the creation of Allah but in the process of being sincere to the creation of Allah, they lose sincerity with Him.

❦ 24 ❦

Your Beautiful Veil

اللَّهُمَّ اسْتُرْنَا بِسِتْرِكَ الجَمِيْلِ،
وَاجْعَلْ تَحْتَ السِّتْرِ مَا تَرْضَى بِهِ عَنَّا

*Allāhumma usturnā bi-sitrika al-jamīli,
waj'al taḥta al-sitri mā-tarḍā bihi 'annā*

**O Allah, veil us with Your beautiful veil and place
beneath that veil what will please You from us.**

A clear subject of most of the supplications of the pious
predecessors is sincerity, which shows where their
priorities lay, but each one gives us something different.
One person asked Allah to excuse their private disgrace
because of the good that they do in public; one asked
Allah to make them a better person than other people
might think of them, and forgive them for what they

don't know, and there are different ways that the Salaf, the pious predecessors, used to verbalize sincerity in their *du'ā*'s.

Sufyan ibn 'Uyaynah *(may Allah be pleased with him)* was a renowned student of Sufyan al-Thawri *(may Allah be pleased with him)*, and he teaches us a *du'ā'* that matches in detail and emotion some of the greatest supplications for sincerity. In his *du'ā'*, Sufyan is not only asking Allah *(glorified and exalted is He)* to not make him a hypocrite, or to allow his private disgrace to ruin his public good, but he is asking Him for deeds that are so good that even the veil won't do it justice. That is why al-Fu'ayl ibn 'Iyad *(may Allah be pleased with him)* said that the pious predecessors used to hide their good deeds with the same vigilance that they hid their sins.

When you reach that point, your good deeds become so precious between you and Allah *(glorified and exalted is He)* that you feel that if someone is gazing into that private devotion they're almost intruding on a beautiful relationship. That's when you know that you are attaining a level of ihsan, a level of excellence where you are starting to enjoy a conversation between you and Allah *(glorified and exalted is He)* that is so private you wouldn't even want your spouse to know. So you save the best for that which no one else sees but Allah *(glorified and exalted is He)*.

🌿 25 🌿

O Teacher of Abraham

يَا مُعَلِّمَ إِبْرَاهِيْمَ عَلِّمْنِي

Yā muʿallima Ibrāhima ʿallimnī

O Teacher of Abraham! Teach me!

━━━━━ ✦ ━━━━━

Some of the most exquisite narrations that we have of *duʿāʾ*'s and practices are from students narrating what they saw from their teachers. If you have ever felt that you were having a hard time understanding something, or you were feeling disconnected from it, or if you are trying to comprehend a verse or hadith and have become stuck, this *duʿāʾ* may help. Imam Ibn Qayyim narrates from his teacher, Imam Ibn Taymiyyah: 'I frequently used to hear him when he would get stuck in his studies, he would make this *du'ā'* and would say, "O Teacher of Abraham! Teach me!'" Some narrations say, 'O He who caused Sulayman *(peace be upon him)* to understand! Make me understand!' This *du'ā'* reminds us that as we are becoming bogged down in things we are trying to understand, recognize that Allah *(glorified and exalted is He)* is the One who grants knowledge, understanding, wisdom and relief.

Beyond the immediate implication of the *du'ā'*, of calling upon Allah *(glorified and exalted is He)* in this way, is the idea that you are connecting yourself to the Lord of the prophets. Often, as you are reading the Qur'an or going through their *du'ā*'s, you forget that the One who helped those prophets and heard them in their darkest times is the same Lord that you call upon. The Lord of Zakariya, of Ibrahim, of Maryam, of 'Isa, and of Muhammad *(may Allah bless them and give them peace)* is your Lord as well. So when you read about the miracles that Allah *(glorified and exalted is He)* worked in their lives, recognize that He could work those same miracles in your life, and when you go through the daily difficulties, trials and struggles which you may go through as you're trying to increase yourself, recognize that you have the Lord of Ibrahim *(peace be upon him)* on your side.

May Allah *(glorified and exalted is He)*, the Lord of the prophets, teach us and grant us the station of the prophets as well. *Āmīn.*

❧ 26 ❧

Your Greatness
— vs —
My Insignificance

اللَّهُمَّ أَنْتَ أَنْتَ وَأَنَا أَنَا: أَنْتَ الْعَوَّادُ بِالْمَغْفِرَةِ
وَأَنَا الْعَوَّادُ بِالذُّنُوبِ فَاغْفِرْ لِي

Allāhumma anta anta wa-anā anā: anta al-ʿawwādu
bil-maghfirati wa-anā al-ʿawwādu bil-dhunūbi fa-ghfir lī

O Allah, You are who You are, and I am who I am;
You are the One who keeps forgiving, and I am the one
who keeps sinning, so forgive me!

This is a narration about a man belonging to the nations that came before us, either from the Children of Israel *(Banū Isrāʿīl)* or the nation that preceded that of the Prophet Muhammad *(peace be upon him)*. It's an authentic narration that some say traces to Jābir *(may Allah be pleased with him)*, who narrates: 'I heard the Prophet *(peace be upon him)* say that there was a man from the nations that came before you, and as he was walking, he came to a moment of regret and called upon Allah. He said the following words: "O Allah, You are who You are, and I am who I am; You are the One who keeps forgiving, and I am the one who keeps sinning, so forgive me!" Then he fell into *sujūd (prostration)*. The Prophet *(peace be upon him)* said that a voice called out to him and said, "you are the one that consistently sins and I am the One that consistently forgives, so I have forgiven you", so he raised his head and Allah *(glorified and exalted is He)* had truly forgiven him.'

It's very clear that when you are calling upon Allah *(glorified and exalted is He)*, you are thinking about poetry or about His names, but sometimes invoking Him in the simplest of ways is a means of attaining forgiveness from Allah *(glorified and exalted is He)* and attaining exactly what you may be asking Him for. Recognize, that when you call upon Him and supplicate He knows your feelings and what you're going to ask of

Him already. You're only trying to articulate in the most loving and perfect way, but the point of the *du'ā'* is not just to make a request but to recognize what takes place in the process of that request, which is connection to Allah *(glorified and exalted is He)* and the realization that comes with that process as well.

O Allah! You are who You are and we are who we are. We are your sinful servants and You are our forgiving Lord, so we ask You to forgive each and every single one of us. *Āmīn.*

*R*ecognize, that
when you call upon
Him and supplicate
He knows your
feelings and what
you're going to ask
of Him already.

27

My Love for You

اللَّهُمَّ إِنَّكَ قَدْ قَبَضْتَ سَهْلاً، وَعَبْدَ المَلِكَ، وَمُزَاحِما، فَلَمْ أَزْدَدْ لَكَ إِلَّا حُبّاً، وَلَا فِيْمَا عِنْدَكَ إِلَّا رَغْبَةً فَاقْبِضْنِي إِلَيْكَ غَيْرَ مُضَيِّعٍ وَلَا مُفَرِّطٍ

Allāhumma innaka qad qabaḍta Sahlan, wa-ʿAbd al-Malika, wa-Muzāḥimā, fa-lam azdad laka illā ḥubban, wa-lā fīmā ʿindaka illā raghbatan faqbiḍnī ilayka ghayra muḍayyiʿin wa-lā mufarriṭin

O Allah, You took back the soul of Sahl, ʿAbd al-Malik, and Muzāḥim, and it only made me love You more, and more desirous of what awaits with You, so take back my soul without me being negligent or careless.

❖

There is probably nothing more difficult that can happen to a person than losing a child. There are many efforts that try to help people cope with the loss of a child, because it truly alters a person's life, and may Allah *(glorified and exalted is He)* bring peace and comfort to all those parents that have lost children and allow their children to bring them into Jannah. *Āmīn*. It's a nightmare that none of us want but the Prophet *(peace be upon him)* went through six times, as he had to bury six of his seven children. How, after burying your wife and six of your seven children in your own lifetime, and with everything else that's going on, do you have the emotional capacity to smile at everyone and still have so much to give to so many people around you?

'Umar ibn 'Abd al-'Aziz *(may Allah be pleased with him)* lost three of his children, Sahl, 'Abd al- Malik, and Muzahim, even though he died barely reaching the age of forty, and he made this profound *du'ā'* to Allah *(glorified and exalted is He)*. 'Umar did not claim that he was not hurt by the loss of his children, it's natural—and the Prophet *(peace be upon him)* himself cried when his children passed away—but what he said was that the loss of his children did not make him resent Allah *(glorified and exalted is He)*, it actually increased his love for Him and made him desire the Hereafter, which

The loss of his children did not make him resent Allah, it actually increased his love for Him and made him desire the Hereafter.

'awaits me with You', even more. He went on, asking Allah *(glorified and exalted is He)* to 'take back my soul' as He took the souls of his children but to not let him be negligent or behave in a way that displeases Him.

If you have suffered from great pain, try to convert that pain into pleasure in the Hereafter. Do not pretend like the pain doesn't exist in this life, it existed in the lives of the Prophet *(peace be upon him)* and great men like 'Umar *(may Allah be pleased with him)*, but instead take that pain and convert it into a request for pleasure in the Hereafter.

May Allah *(glorified and exalted is He)* protect our children, comfort the parents who have lost their children, and have mercy on those children. May He gather those parents with their children in Jannat al-Firdaws and allow all the tragedies that we face in this life only increase our love for Him and the desire for the Hereafter. *Āmīn.*

28

Record Me Among the Blessed

اللَّهُمَّ إِنْ كُنْتَ كَتَبْتَنِي فِي أَهْلِ السَّعَادَةِ فَأَثْبِتْنِي فِيهَا وَإِنْ كُنْتَ كَتَبْتَ عَلَيَّ الذَّنْبَ وَالشِّقْوَةَ فَامْحُنِي وَأَثْبِتْنِي فِي أَهْلِ السَّعَادَةِ فَإِنَّكَ تَمْحُو مَا تَشَاءُ وَتُثْبِتُ وَعِنْدَكَ أُمُّ الْكِتَابِ

Allāhumma in kunta katabtanī fī ahli al-saʿādati fa-athbitnī fīhā, wa-in kunta katabta ʿalayya al-dhanba wash-shiqwata famḥunī wa-athbitnī fī ahli al-saʿādati fa'innaka tamḥū mā-tashā'u wa-tuthbitu wa-ʿindaka ummu al-kitābi

O Allah, if You have recorded me among the blessed, then affirm it therein, and if You have recorded me among the sinful and the damned, then wipe it away and affirm me among the blessed. Verily, You wipe away and affirm whatever You will, and with You is the mother of the Book.

———— ✦ ————

Abū 'Uthman al-Hindi *(may Allah be pleased with him)* records this incident where he was doing tawaf around the Ka'bah and he says, 'I noticed 'Umar ibn Khattāb doing tawaf also', and in the middle of his tawaf 'Umar suddenly started to weep. 'Uthman says, 'I walked close to 'Umar while he was weeping to hear what he was saying', and he overheard the following *du'ā*': 'O Allah, if You have recorded me among the blessed, then affirm it therein, and if You have recorded me among the sinful and the damned, then wipe it away and affirm me among the blessed. Verily, You wipe away and affirm what You will, and with You is the mother of the Book.'

This *du'ā*' once again speaks of 'Umar's fear that his name is on the list of hypocrites, even though the Prophet *(peace be upon him)* affirmed many times that 'Umar *(may Allah be pleased with him)* was guaranteed Paradise.

The Prophet *(peace be upon him)* said that as you come into this world, after four months in the womb of your mother the angels write not just your life-span, your *rizq (sustenance),* and your date of death, but they write down whether you will be *saʿīd (fortunate)* or *shaqī (deprived).* That does not mean that you cannot change your fate and your fortune, or that you are stuck in some sort of damnation or deprivation. However, ʿUmar *(may Allah be pleased with him)* was speaking about the scrolls held by Allah *(glorified and exalted is He),* and this is the best way to understand your position with Allah *(glorified and exalted is He).*

In terms of your scrolls, Allah says that on the Day of Judgement everyone will receive their book of deeds either in their right hand or their left hand, and may Allah *(glorified and exalted is He)* make us among those who receive their scrolls in their right hands. Some people will celebrate, they will go around showing their record to everyone; others will try to hide their scroll, but they will be chained with their left hand behind their back holding their book of deeds. Hence, the question arises: if Allah were to give you your book of deeds right now, would you be comfortable enough to show it to others? That's what ʿUmar *(may Allah be pleased with him)* is talking about, and he is teaching us here—besides the lessons and understanding of Divine decree—to act practically upon this *duʿāʾ*. If Allah *(glorified and exalted is He)* were to give you your book of deeds now, would He give it to your right hand or your left hand? And if He were to give it to your left hand, what would you need to do to wipe away those deeds?

May Allah *(glorified and exalted is He)* record us among those who are affirmed in happiness and righteousness, and may He affirm now that we are recorded on that list. May Allah allow the homes that He has made for us in Paradise remain our homes and not let others inherit them, and may He protect us from the Fire and from being recorded amongst the deprived and those who have earned His displeasure. *Āmīn.*

❦ 29 ❦

Beautify
My Character

اللَّهُمَّ كَمَا حَسَّنْتَ خَلْقِي فَحَسِّنْ خُلُقِي

Allāhumma kamā ḥassanta khalqī faḥassin khuluqī

**O Allah, as You have beautified my external
appearance then beautify my character.**

---✦---

U mm al-Dardā' *(may Allah be pleased with her)*
narrates, 'I saw my husband, Abū al-Dardā', praying
throughout the night and making a single supplication'.
He was praying the *duʿā'* of the Prophet *(peace be upon
him)*: 'O Allah, as You have beautified my external
appearance then beautify my character.' Your *khalq* is
your physical appearance, and your *khuluq* represents
your character, which is your internal appearance.

Imagine if you could have an image of your character, what would it look like if you held it up to a mirror, and that's really what this *duʿāʾ* speaks of. But why would Abū al-Dardāʾ *(may Allah be pleased with him)* spend the entire night making this *duʿāʾ*, asking for nothing except for good character?

In the morning, Umm al-Dardāʾ *(may Allah be pleased with her)* asked her husband, 'why did you not ask from Allah anything else than good character?' He replied, 'O Umm al-Dardāʾ! Verily a Muslim beautifies his character, and as a result of that he treats people so well that they make *duʿāʾ* for him *(they supplicate for him)* until he enters Jannah because of their prayers. And a Muslim who corrupts his character until he hurts someone due to that bad character, then someone supplicates against him and he enters Hellfire as a result of that.' Therefore, the only thing that Abū al-Dardāʾ *(may Allah be pleased with him)* wished for was good character, because if that character is genuine and sincere, not only does it mean that he had a genuine connection with Allah *(glorified and exalted is He)* but because of the goodness in himself, everyone that he came into contact with will testify in his favour on the Day of Judgement.

As he was passing away, Abū Dujānah *(may Allah be pleased with him)* was asked what made him most hopeful regarding his relationship with Allah *(glorified and exalted is He)*. Was it the great deeds that he had done, that he was a warrior who fought alongside the Prophet *(peace be upon him)* on many occasions: 'you grabbed him on the day of Uhud and your back was covered with arrows to the point that you looked like a hedgehog, so what makes you most hopeful for receiving the mercy of Allah?' He replied, 'nothing makes me more hopeful for the mercy of Allah except that I never used this tongue to hurt anyone.' Subhan Allah.

May Allah *(glorified and exalted is He)* give us good character and may He allow that character to not just be true to His creation but allow it to be a reflection of our sincerity towards our Creator. May He help us not to hurt anyone knowingly or unknowingly so that they testify against us on the Day of Judgement and hurt us or cause us doom, and forgive us for the harm that we do, either knowingly or unknowingly. Help us control our tongue and other parts in transgressing others' lives, property and honour, knowingly or unknowingly, and may Allah *(glorified and exalted is He)* enter us into Jannah by His mercy and our good character. *Āmīn*.

Nothing makes me more hopeful for the mercy of Allah except that I never used this tongue to hurt anyone.

Show Us
Guidance and Error

اللَّهُمَّ أَرِنِي الحَقَّ حَقّاً وَوَفِّقْنِي لِاتِّبَاعِهِ،
وَأَرِنِي البَاطِلَ بَاطِلاً وَوَفِّقْنِي لِاجْتِنَابِهِ

*Allāhumma arinī al-ḥaqqa ḥaqqan wa-waffiqnī
littibāʿihī, wa-arinī al-bāṭila bāṭilan
wa-waffiqnī lijtinābihi*

O Allah, show me the truth as truth,
and guide me to follow it; and show me
the false as false, and guide me to avoid it.

❖

As we have been reading through these different prayers, they may raise questions in your mind: How do I know what the truth is? How do I know what Allah really wants from me? How do I know that I'm upon the path that will allow me to enter into Jannah and earn me that mercy? If you look at *surah al-Fātihah*, there is a prayer for guidance, and it seems fitting to end this book with such a prayer. First and foremost, you should understand that there is no way that you're going to ask Allah sincerely for guidance seventeen times a day and He leads you astray. If you are sincere in asking for guidance from Allah then most certainly He will guide you to the right path; ask Allah for guidance, ask Him for *hidāyah*. That's what made this *du'ā'* from 'Umar *(may Allah be pleased with him)* so special.

You might be doing something that feels right but it's not actually guidance and righteousness, or you might be engaging in something that you're not so sure about. Sometimes, you hear different people telling you different things about how to get close to Allah *(glorified and exalted is He)* and you're unsure. Hence, the most important *du'ā'* to always keep in mind is that for guidance: Guide us to understand Your message properly; guide us to practise the Sunnah of Your Prophet *(peace be upon him)* properly; guide us to see our faults and our shortcomings. Guide us so that we do not unknowingly take a path that leads us away from You. So I hope, *inshā' Allāhu ta'ālā*, that you have benefitted from this book and from the prayers of the Salaf, and that you don't forget these *du'ā's* and this particular prayer.

May Allah *(glorified and exalted is He)* allow us to be upon the path of guidance and to guide others. May He never let us stray by the actions of the accursed devil or by the lowliness of ourselves, and may Allah *(glorified and exalted is He)* allow that path of guidance to result in a path to Paradise and entering into His mercy on the Day of Judgement. *Āmīn.*

My Prayer Journal

Use this section to note down your personal du'ās. You may wish to use the keywords for inspiration.

PRAYER NOTES	KEYWORDS
My Lord, ...	*Forgiveness*
....	*Hope*
....	*Paradise*
....	*The Hereafter*
....	*Forever*
....	
....	
....	

PRAYER NOTES	KEYWORDS
O Creator, ...	*Mercy*
....	*Devotion*
....	*Need*
....	*Shortcomings*
....	*Reliance*
....	
....	
....	
O Provider, ...	*Heart*
....	*Desire*
....	*Living*
....	*Provision*
....	*Dreams*
....	
....	
....	

PRAYER NOTES	KEYWORDS
O Merciful Lord, ...	*Dedication*
....	*Light*
....	*Longing*
....	*Sweetness*
....	*Sacrifice*
....	
....	
....	
My Master, ...	*Wishes*
....	*Increase*
....	*Witness*
....	*Good deeds*
....	*Belief*
....	
....	
....	

PRAYER NOTES   **KEYWORDS**

O Guardian Lord, ...   *Grateful*

....   *Certainty*

....   *Ease*

....   *Kindness*

....   *Provision*

....

....

....

O Protector, ...   *Generous*

....   *Future*

....   *Joyful*

....   *Discover*

....   *Blessings*

....

....

....

PRAYER NOTES   KEYWORDS

O Almighty Lord, ...   *Success*

....   *Admission*

....   *Revival*

....   *My flaws*

....   *Promise*

....

....

....

O Turner of Hearts, ...   *Surrender*

....   *Your Glory*

....   *Beautiful*

....   *Dedication*

....   *Character*

....

....

....

PRAYER NOTES	KEYWORDS
O Forgiving Lord, ...	*Goodness*
....	*Witness*
....	*Purity*
....	*Striving*
....	*Prayer*
....	
....	
....	
O Giver of Life, ...	*Reminder*
....	*Sacrifice*
....	*Confidence*
....	*Peace*
....	*Future*
....	
....	
....